The International Highrise Award 2014
Internationaler Hochhaus Preis 2014

Herausgegeben von **Edited by**
Peter Körner und **and** Peter Cachola Schmal

Statements der Juroren
Statements of the jurors

„Bosco Verticale ist ein wunderbares Projekt! Er ist Ausdruck des alles umfassenden menschlichen Bedürfnisses nach Grün."
"Bosco Verticale is a wonderful project! It is an expression of the overall human need of green."

„Das Projekt beantwortet äußerst komplexe Fragen der internationalen Architektur und sämtliche Probleme, die wir mit der Verdichtung, mit dem Bau von Hochhäusern in den Städten für eine wachsende Zahl von Menschen und mit ihren elementaren Bedürfnissen nach frischer Luft und Naturnähe haben. Es bietet den Bewohnern einen Balkon oder eine Terrasse und eine kleine Wohnung mit herrlicher Aussicht. Die Konzentration auf die Komplexität des Projekts, die Konzentration auf die Fassade und auf die Beziehung zwischen Innen und Außen ist ein wunderbarer Umgang mit Architektur."
"The project brings down very complex questions of international architecture and all the issues we have about density, about building highrises in cities for a growing number of people and their very basic needs like fresh air or contact to nature. It provides a balcony or an outside terrace and shelters people in a small apartment with a beautiful view. The concentration of the complexity of the project, the concentration on the façade and on the issues of the relation of inside and the outside is a wonderful approach to architecture."
Christoph Ingenhoven, ingenhoven architects, Juryvorsitz **Chairman of the jury**, *Düsseldorf*

„Eine radikale Idee, passend für die radikalen europäischen Städter von morgen!"
"A radical idea fit for the radical European urbanites of tomorrow!"
Peter Cachola Schmal, Direktor **Director** *Deutsches Architekturmuseum, Frankfurt am Main*

„Wie ungemein italienisch! Dank der versetzten Balkone kann man mit seinen Nachbarn in Kontakt treten."
"How sweetly Italian! You can connect with your neighbours thanks to the offset balconies."
Yew-Thong Leong, Professor für Architektur **Professor of architecture**, *Ryerson University, Toronto*

„Die Art, wie das Gebäude eine Wiederbegrünung der Stadt ermöglicht, könnte definitiv zum Vorbild für die Bebauung dichter Gebiete in anderen europäischen Städten werden."
"The way the building enabled a re-greening of the city could definitely become a role model for development of dense areas in other European cities."
Louisa Hutton, Sauerbruch Hutton, Berlin

„In der Regel wird Technologie eingesetzt, um Klimaprobleme zu lösen. Hier haben wir einen Rückgriff auf die Natur, sodass die Natur selbst die Probleme löst."
"Customarily, technology is deployed to solve climate issues. Here, we have a re-connect with nature so that nature itself solves the problems."
Swantje Kühn, GKK+Architekten, Berlin

„Eine großartige bio-inspirierte Architektur als Lowtech-Methode, um das innerstädtische Mikroklima mit geeigneten Mitteln auf eine Weise zu verbessern, die wahrhaft bahnbrechend sein könnte."
"A great bio-inspired architecture as a low-tech method for improving downtown microclimates using appropriate means in a manner that could blaze a real trail."
Jan Knippers, Professor für Tragkonstruktionen und Konstruktives Entwerfen **Professor of Building Structures and Structural Design**, *Universität Stuttgart*

Bosco Verticale, Mailand **Milan**, Italien **Italy**
Gewinner des Internationalen Hochhaus Preises 2014
Winner of the International Highrise Award 2014

Das von der Jury einstimmig zum Sieger gewählte Hochhaus ist der Bosco Verticale in Mailand der Architekten Boeri Studio und des Bauherrn Hines Italia SGR S.p.A.

Die Jury war überaus angetan von der Art und Weise, wie dieses Hochhaus leistet, was Architektur leisten soll. Es bietet auf ehrliche Art Schutz und Raum, bezieht zugleich Natur, Licht und Luft ein und bringt damit die menschlichen Grundbedürfnisse in ein ausgewogenes Verhältnis. Dabei ist es nicht komplexer als nötig. Der Bosco Verticale zeugt von Mut zur Veränderung, da die Bäume und Sträucher auf versetzten Balkonen wachsen, die eine höchst lebendige Fassade bilden und die der Juror Neil Thomas mit Gartenzäunen in der Luft verglich, über die hinweg man plaudern kann. Somit sind sie ein kommunikatives Element und beugen Anonymität vor. Diese Balkone verschmelzen zu einem Garten, und so können Bewohner sogar ein Schlafzimmer zum Garten haben – mitten in Mailand!

Die Jury war zudem überzeugt, dass die Balkone ein architektonisches Mittel sind, das sich überall einsetzen lässt, und dass sie daher einen echten Prototyp darstellen – Großflächig angewendet könnte diese Lowtech-Methode das innerstädtische Mikroklima derart verbessern, dass diese Form von bio-inspirierter Architektur zum Standard der Zukunft werden könnte.

Die Jury kam zu dem Schluss, dass der Bosco Verticale Landschaftsgestaltung in das Gebäude holt und dadurch auch die CO_2-Bilanz positiv beeinflusst. Auf aufwendige Technik zur Lösung klimatischer Herausforderungen kann hier verzichtet werden, da deren Aufgaben von der Natur übernommen werden. Gleichzeitig erfolgt eine Wiederaufforstung der Stadt, die in diesem Umfang zum Vorbild für andere dichte Städte in Europa avancieren könnte. Kulturdezernent Prof. Dr. Felix Semmelroth fasste zusammen: „Das ist ein dramatischer Prototyp, der nach meiner festen Überzeugung die Stadtplanungsdiskussionen und die Debatten über Wohnhochhäuser in Städten wie Frankfurt voranbringen wird."

The winning highrise, chosen by unanimous jury vote, was Bosco Verticale in Milan, Italy, by architects Boeri Studio and commissioned by Hines Italia SGR S.p.A.

The jury was very taken by the way the highrise does what architecture is supposed to do. It is very honest in providing shelter and space, while at the same time introducing nature, light and air, and thus balancing the key principles of human needs. It is at the same time no more complex than it should be. Bosco Verticale exhibits the courage to embrace change, as the trees and plants grow on the staggered balconies that form its highly animated façade, which jury member Neil Thomas compared to creating garden fences in the air to chat across. Fellow jury member Yew-Thong Leong commented: "How sweetly Italian. You can connect with your neighbours thanks to the offset balconies." These balconies morph into a garden, so that residents can even have their bedrooms next to the garden – in downtown Milan.

Furthermore, the jury was convinced that the balconies are an architectural device which can be employed anywhere and which therefore represent a true prototype. When used over large areas, this low-tech method could improve the microclimate of the city centre so dramatically that this type of biologically inspired architecture could become a standard for the future.

The jury concluded that the Bosco Verticale brings landscaping into the building while "through this very device also impacting favourably on the carbon footprint". As Jury member Swantje Kühn put it, "Customarily, technology is deployed to solve climate issues. Here, we have a re-connect with nature so that nature itself solves the problems." Louisa Hutton was taken by the way the building enabled a re-greening of the city in a way that could definitely become a role model for development of dense areas in other European cities. Deputy Mayor Prof Dr Felix Semmelroth summarized that this "is a dramatic prototype that will, I am sure, advance urban planning discussions and debates on residential highrises in cities such as Frankfurt."

Gewinner 2014 **Prize Winner 2014**

Boeri Studio
BOSCO VERTICALE
Mailand **Milan**, Italien **Italy**

Architekten **Architects** Boeri Studio, Mailand **Milan**
Entwurfsarchitekten **Design architects** Stefano Boeri,
Gianandrea Barreca, Giovanni La Varra
Leitende Architekten **Executive architects** Davor
Popovic, Francesco de Felice
Projektarchitekten **Project architects** Phase 1
(Städtebau und Entwurf **Urban planning and schematic
design**) Frederic de Smet (Koordination **Coordination**),
Daniele Barillari, Julien Boitard, Matilde Cassani,
Andrea Casetto, Francesca Cesa Bianchi, Inge
Lengwenus, Corrado Longa, Eleanna Kotsikou, Matteo
Marzi, Emanuela Messina, Andrea Sellanes
Projektarchitekten **Project architects** Phase 2
(Ausführungsplanung **Execution planning**) Gianni
Bertoldi (Koordination **Coordination**), Alessandro Agosti,
Marco Brega, Andrea Casetto, Matteo Colognese,
Angela Parrozzani, Stefano Onnis
Bauherr **Client** Hines Italia SGR S.p.A.
Tragwerksplanung **Structural engineers** Arup Italia Srl
Haustechnik **MEP** Deerns Italia S.p.A.
Ausführungsplanung **Execution planning** Tekne Srl
Grünplanung Gebäude **Botanical consultant** Emanuela
Borio, Laura Gatti
Landschaftsarchitekten **Landscape architects** Land Srl

Höhe **Height** Turm **Tower** D 78 m, Turm **Tower** E 122 m
Geschosse **Floors** Turm **Tower** D 18, Turm **Tower** E 24
Grundstücksfläche **Site area** 75 782 m²
Bebaute Fläche **Footprint** Turm **Tower** E 675 m², Turm
Tower D 500 m²
Bruttogeschossfläche mit Terrassen und Balkonen **Total
floor area incl. terraces and balconies**
Turm **Tower** E 18 717 m² + 3280 m², Turm **Tower** D
9412 m² + 1600 m²
Nettogeschossfläche **Net floor area** Turm **Tower** E
16 011 m², Turm **Tower** D 8045 m²
Konstruktion **Structure** Stahlbeton **Reinforced concrete**
Fertigstellung **Completion** Juni **June** 2014
Nutzung **Use** Wohnen **Residential**
Ökologische Aspekte / Nachhaltigkeit **Ecological
criteria / sustainability** Die intensive Bepflanzung der
Fassaden führt zur: Absorbierung von Staub und CO₂,
Produktion von Sauerstoff, Verbesserung des Mikroklimas, Verschattung der Balkone und Wohnungen,
dadurch Energieeinsparungen; nachhaltige Stadtentwicklung durch Verdichtung sowie Begrünung des
Stadtraums. **The large number of plants on the
façades leads to the absorption of dust and carbon
dioxide, they produce oxygen and improve the
microclimate, they provide shade for the balconies and
flats, thereby saving energy; sustainable urban
development results from creating a compact urban
space and providing green space in the city.**

Blick von Bosco Verticale auf den Palazzo Lombardia, den
Regierungs- und Verwaltungssitz der Lombardei von Pei Cobb
Freed & Partners mit dem Logo der Expo 2015.
**View of the Palazzo Lombardia from the Bosco Verticale:
The main seat of the government of Lombardy, designed by
Pei Cobb Freed & Partners, bears the logo of the Expo 2015.**

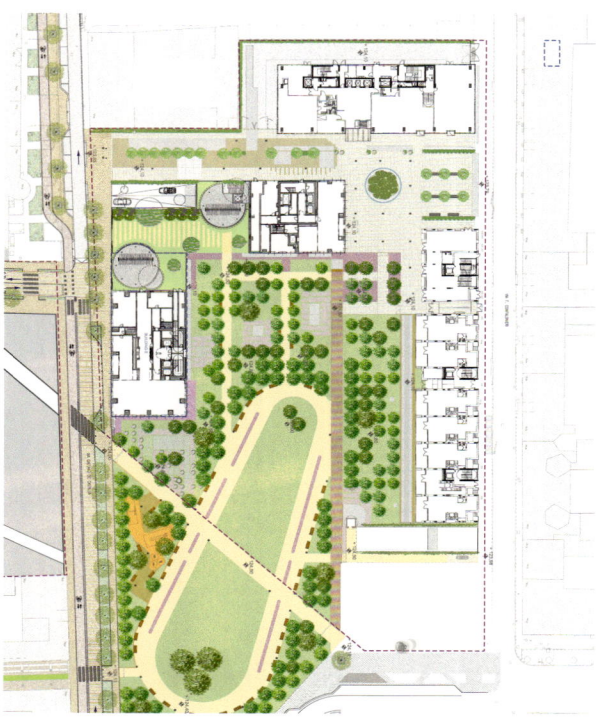

Lageplan mit Grundriss Erdgeschoss
Site plan with ground floor plan

Regelgeschoss Turm D + E
Typical floor plan Tower D + E

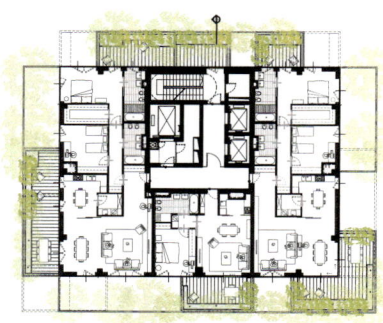

Schnitt Turm D und Nordansicht Turm E
Section Tower D and north elevation Tower E

Durch die raumhohen Fenster haben die
Bewohner sowohl einen Ausblick in die Natur als
auch über die Dächer von Mailand.
The floor-to-ceiling windows offer residents a
view into nature as well as over the rooftops of
Milan.

In einem Park zwischen der Via Gaetano de Castilla und der Via Federico Confalonieri im Norden Mailands stehen zwei an ihren Außenfassaden begrünte Wohnhochhäuser. Sie sind Teil eines Revitalisierungsprojekts der Stadt Mailand, die mit ihrem Programm „Metrobosco" eine Verdichtung des Stadtgebietes unter umweltverträglichen Bedingungen vorsieht.

Zur Bebauung des 75 782 Quadratmeter großen Grundstücks gehören außer den beiden Wohnhochhäusern noch ein Bürohochhaus und eine Blockrandbebauung entlang der Via Federico Confalonieri. Allerdings sind nur die Wohnhochhäuser begrünt. Sie basieren auf rechteckigen Grundrissen und sind mit 18 (Turm D) bzw. 24 (Turm E) Stockwerken unterschiedlich hoch. Die um einen zentralen Gebäudekern mit Aufzügen und Treppenhaus angeordneten Stockwerksplatten kragen unregelmäßig über die Fassaden aus. Dort bilden sie Terrassen und Balkone, die mit Pflanzen und Bäumen bestückt sind. So erhält jede der 400 unterschiedlich großen Wohnungen Zugang zu mindestens einer Terrasse oder einem Balkon. In luftiger Höhe haben die Bewohner ihren eigenen Garten – besser gesagt: ihr kleines Waldstück. Denn es sind an die 900 Bäume, die an den Fassaden wachsen, durchmischt mit Stauden, Sträuchern und blühenden Bodendeckern. Die weit gefächerte Pflanzenvielfalt entspricht pro Hochhaus derjenigen eines ganzen Hektar Waldes.

Durch die intensive Bepflanzung entstanden zusätzliche Lasten. Die Bodenplatten mussten mit Stahl armiert werden, was zu einer Dicke von 28 Zentimetern führte. An den Außenkanten werden die Terrassen von Pflanzkästen begrenzt, die mit einer Höhe von 1,30 Metern zugleich als Brüstungen dienen. Auch erhöhten sich die Baukosten durch die Vorkehrungen für die Begrünung um fünf Prozent. Die Mehrkosten werden jedoch langfristig wieder ausgeglichen, denn das naturnahe Wohnen wird nicht mit Hilfe von aufwendiger Technik, sondern durch die Pflanzen selbst erreicht. Diese sorgen für ein angenehmes Mikroklima, absorbieren Partikel und Staub aus der Luft, verarbeiten Kohlendioxid und wandeln dieses wieder in Sauerstoff und Luftfeuchte um. Sie dienen als Sonnenschutz während der heißen Sommermonate und tragen zu Energieeinsparungen bei. Und sie können mit Grauwasser, dem Abwasser aus dem Gebäude, versorgt werden.

Unter Hinzuziehung von Botanikern und Gärtnern wurden die Pflanzen für ihre jeweilige Position an der Fassade ausgewählt und herangezüchtet. Ihre Pflege wie auch ein ausgefeiltes Bewässerungssystem sind Teil des Gesamtkonzepts. Als Pionierprojekt im Rahmen von „Metrobosco" sind die „bewaldeten Hochhäuser" ein anschauliches Beispiel einer Symbiose von Architektur und Natur.

Two residential highrises with green façades stand in a park between Via Gaetano de Castilla and Via Federico Confalonieri in the north of Milan. They are part of the revitalization project of Milan, whose programme "Metrobosco" aims to create a compacter city while adhering to environmental principles.

In addition to these two residential highrises, the 75,782 square metre site also contains an office highrise and a perimeter row of buildings along Via Federico Confalonieri. However, only the residential buildings have green façades. They have rectangular ground-plans and are of different heights, 18 (Tower D) and 24 (Tower E) floors respectively. The floors, arranged around a central core with elevators and stairs, protrude in an irregular fashion beyond the façades, where they create terraces and balconies planted with shrubs and trees. Every one of the 400 differently sized flats thus has access to at least one terrace or balcony. In lofty heights the residents have their own garden, or rather, their own little woodland, for the buildings are covered in around 900 trees, interspersed with shrubs, bushes and flowering groundcover. The diverse flora on each highrise is equivalent to that of an entire hectare of forest.

The sheer weight of plants creates additional loads. The concrete floor slabs had to be reinforced with steel, which resulted in a thickness of twenty-eight centimetres. Around the exterior perimeter, the terraces are lined with planters, which, with a height of 1.30 metres, also function as a balustrade. The construction costs were also five percent higher as a result of the extra measures taken for the green façades. But these additional costs will be made up for later, because living in these green buildings is not a matter of elaborate technology; the plants themselves do the work. They create a pleasant microclimate, absorb particles and dust from the air, process carbon dioxide and turn it into oxygen and humidity again. They provide sun protection during the hot summer months and contribute to energy savings. In addition, they can be kept alive using the buildings' grey water.

The plants were selected and bred for their respective final positions on the façade following consultation with botanists and gardeners. Their care as well as an ingenious irrigation system are part of the overall concept. As a pioneer project as part of "Metrobosco" the "forested highrises" are a vivid example of a symbiosis between architecture and nature.

Durch den barrierefreien Austritt auf die
Balkone entsteht ein fließender Übergang
zwischen Innen und Außen.
The barrier-free exits onto the balconies
provide a smooth transition between the
interior and exterior spaces.

Der Kontext von Bosco Verticale
Peter Cachola Schmal Direktor, Deutsches
Architekturmuseum, Frankfurt am Main

Das Wohnhochhausprojekt Bosco Verticale in Mailands Stadtumbauquartier Porta Nuova, zwischen dem Bahnhof Porta Garibaldi im Nordwesten und dem Hauptbahnhof Milano Centrale gelegen, überzeugte die Jury des diesjährigen Internationalen Hochhaus Preises gleich auf mehreren Ebenen, nicht nur auf der Objekt-ebene des eigentlichen Gebäudes. Neben der hohen skulpturalen Qualität und innovativ „grünen" Konzeption beeindrucken die Doppeltürme von Stefano Boeri mit ihren High-End-Apartments ab 65 Quadratmetern Größe auch kontextuell. Die Eingangsbereiche sind zweigeschossig ausgelegt und bieten den Bewohnern neben der Rezeption auch eine Lobby mit einem Bereich für gemeinschaftliche Nutzungen. So geht der künftige Park visuell großzügig und direkt in die Türme über und wird mit der Bepflanzung in der Vertikalen weitergeführt.

The context of Bosco Verticale
Peter Cachola Schmal, Director, Deutsches
Architekturmuseum, Frankfurt am Main

The residential highrise project Bosco Verticale in Milan's redevelopment district Porta Nuova, located between Porta Garibaldi station in the northwest and Milano Centrale, the city's main train station, won over the jury of this year's International Highrise Award on several counts, not only as regards the actual building itself. Alongside the immense sculptural quality and innovative "green" concept, the twin towers by Stefano Boeri with their high-end apartments of 65 square metres plus are also convincing in terms of context. The entrance areas are arranged over two floors and not only offer residents a reception, but also a lobby with an area for communal use. When completed, the park will open up and merge with the towers and will be continued in the vertical plane with the vegetation.

Rendering des Stadtquartiers Porta Nuova mit dem Bosco Verticale sowie dem Park „La Biblioteca degli alberi", geplant von Inside Outside aus Amsterdam.
Rendering of the Porta Nuova district with the Bosco Verticale and "La Biblioteca degli alberi" park, designed by Amsterdam-based Inside Outside.

Das satte Grün des Bosco Verticale überragt
die umliegende Bebauung Mailands.
The rich greenery of the Bosco Verticale
towers above the surrounding buildings of
Milan.

Herausragend ist die umfassende Planung ihrer Bepflanzung, die von der differenzierten Auswahl in Bezug auf die jahreszeitliche Varianz und Höhenstaffelung bis hin zu den baulichen Konsequenzen im Detail konsequent umgesetzt wurde. Insgesamt wurden auf den beiden Türmen 480 große und mittlere sowie 250 kleinere Bäume, 14 000 bodenbedeckende Pflanzen und 5000 Büsche gepflanzt. Das entspricht zwei Hektar typischer Waldbepflanzung und rechtfertigt den Namen „Vertikaler Wald". Die mikroklimatischen Vorteile einer umfangreichen Flora am Bauwerk leuchten ein: Die Erhöhung des Sauerstoffgehalts durch fotosynthetische Umwandlung von Kohlendioxid geht einher mit einer Erhöhung der Luftfeuchtigkeit. Staub wird gebunden, die Bewohner werden vor Lärm und Sonnenlicht geschützt und sogar die Fauna wird umfassend (wenn auch unvorhersehbar) bereichert und somit die Biodiversität signifikant erhöht. All dies hatte Boeri bereits 2011 in seinem Plädoyer für eine neue Metropole der Biodiversität, „Biomilano", ausführlich dargelegt. Theoretisch war dies nachvollziehbar, nur praktisch konnte man Fragen wie diese für unser Klima bisher nicht beantworten: Wie hält ein neun Meter hoher Baum in 100 Metern Höhe einem Sturm stand? Wie garantiert man die Sicherheit der Bewohner und Passanten vor eventuell herabstürzenden Bäumen? Wie wird Bewässerung und Pflege, Schnitt und Kontrolle der vielen Bäume und Büsche auf Dauer gesichert? Bei dem Pionierprojekt Bosco Verticale wurde in Zusammenarbeit mit der Botanikerin Laura Gatti echte Grundlagenforschung zur urbanen Begrünung geleistet. Anhand von Windtunneltests am Politecnico di Milano, wo Boeri Professor ist, konnte die Standfestigkeit der Bäume auch bei Orkanen mit Hilfe einer unsichtbar eingebauten Haltekonstruktion der Wurzelballen in speziellen Pflanzbehältern nachgewiesen werden. Für den Bauherrn eine wesentliche Absicherung.

Besonders die Dimension und Beschaffenheit der speziellen Gartenbalkonschicht vor der eher konventionellen Fassade aus Verglasung und gedämmten Metallpaneelen wird von der Jury als gestalterischer Höhepunkt dieses Projekts geschätzt. Denn die versetzte Staffelung und Anordnung dieser ungewöhnlich großzügigen Terrassenbalkone mit ihren enormen Tiefen von 1,83 Metern plus 1,50 Meter breiten Pflanztrögen erzeugt eine räumlich wirkungsvolle, visuell geschützte Zwischenschicht zwischen den Innenräumen und der Außenwelt. Direkt an der Terrassentür wird die Bepflanzung etwas reduziert, um sogar 2,50 Meter tiefe Flächen zu schaffen. Platz genug für einen Sechser-Tisch! Bis zu vier oder fünf Geschosse reicht dieser neuartige Zwischenraum hinauf und beim Blick hinab auch hinunter – eine wohltuende Weite. Die High-End-Apartments sind fast alle 65, 95 oder 135 Quadratmeter groß und jede einzelne Wohnung bietet eine solche Balkonterrasse von 22 bis 80 Quadratmeter. Trotz einem starken Einbruch im Immobilienmarkt aufgrund der Wirtschaftskrise seit 2009 verläuft der Verkauf der Wohnungen, bei niedrigeren Preisen als früher antizipiert, einigermaßen zufriedenstellend. Es sind hauptsächlich Familien aus Mailand, die diese Wohnungen kaufen, selten andere italienische oder ausländische Investoren. Die Preise liegen derzeit bei 2000 Euro Kaltmiete für eine 77 Quadratmeter-Wohnung oder einem Kaufpreis von einer Million Euro für eine 137 Quadratmeter-Wohnung.

Not only was the planning for the greenery in the highrise excellently managed; it was also implemented meticulously and consistently, from the discriminating selection in terms of seasonal variation and staggering heights to the architectural consequences. In all, 480 large and medium-sized and 250 smaller trees, 14,000 floral plants providing ground cover and 5,000 shrubs were planted on the two towers. This corresponds to two hectares of typical forest growth and justifies the name "Vertical Forest". There are obvious benefits for the microclimate in having such extensive greenery on a building: oxygen production is increased thanks to the conversion of carbon dioxide by photosynthesis and this also results in increased humidity. Dust is filtered, the occupants are protected from noise and harsh sunlight, and even the fauna is greatly enriched (though exactly how cannot be predicted), while biodiversity is significantly enhanced. Boeri had already presented all of these ideas in detail back in 2011 in his plea for a new metropolis of biodiversity, "Biomilano". Though his concepts made sense in theory, it has not been possible until now to answer questions such as: How does a six-meter-tall tree planted at a height of 100 meters withstand a storm? How do you ensure residents and passersby remain safe and are not injured by trees falling down? How do you ensure the irrigation, care, pruning and control of many trees and shrubs over the long term? In the pioneering Bosco Verticale project, research was conducted into urban tree planting in collaboration with botanist Laura Gatti. Thanks to wind-tunnel testing at Politecnico di Milano, where Boeri is a professor, it was possible to prove the trees would remain stable even during storms. The solution was to use invisible root-stabilizing structures in the special containers the trees stand in. These measures represent a considerable safeguard for the clients.

As the highlight of the project, the jury especially underlined the size and nature of the special garden balcony level in front of the rather conventional glazed façade with insulated metal panels. After all, the staggering and arrangement of these unusually generous terraces with their enormous depths of 1.83 metres plus 1.50-metre-wide plant tubs create a spatially impressive and private intermediate layer between the interior and exterior. There is somewhat less greenery at the terrace doors to create areas with depths of no less than 2.50 metres. Space enough for a table to seat six people! This innovative intermediate space extends over four or five floors, and creates an agreeable sense of openness when you look up or down. Almost all the high-end apartments measure 65, 95 or 135 square metres and each individual apartment also has such a terrace covering 22 to 80 square metres. Despite a slump in the real-estate market owing to the economic crisis that began in 2009, the sale of the apartments is proceeding reasonably well, albeit at lower prices. It is mostly families from Milan who are buying, seldom other Italian or foreign investors. Current prices are EUR 2,000 basic monthly rent exclusive of heating, water, etc. for a 77-square-metre apartment, or EUR 1 million to buy a 137-square-metre apartment.

Der Luftraum über den Balkonen variiert. So
finden Bäume mit einer Höhe von bis zu neun
Metern Platz.
The air space above the balconies varies,
providing space for trees up to nine
metres high.

Auch die städtebaulichen Vorzüge, wie der geringe Flächenverbrauch überzeugen. Denn jeder Turm entspricht in seiner Bevölkerungsdichte einem Gebiet von 50 000 Quadratmetern Einfamilienhausbebauung und spart zusätzlich den potenziellen Pendlerverkehr ein. Auf der stadträumlichen Ebene gehört das Viertel Porta Nuova als erfolgreich realisierter Baustein zur umfassenden Umgestaltung von Mailand nach einem jahrzehntelangen ökonomischen Abschwung, der einen Rückgang der Einwohnerzahlen von über 1,7 Millionen in den 1970er-Jahren zu heute etwa 1,3 Millionen, aufgrund einer Wanderbewegung an die Peripherie und zu neuen Satellitenstädten, zur Folge hatte. Die städtebauliche Weiterentwicklung kulminiert in der Weltausstellung Expo Milano 2015 mit dem Slogan „Den Planeten ernähren. Energie fürs Leben" (Feeding the Planet. Energy for Life). Verantwortlich für den Masterplan der Expo zeichnen Ricky Burdett (von der London School of Economics), Jaques Herzog (von Baseler Architekturbüro Herzog de Meuron) und Stefano Boeri. Die Expo (vom 1. Mai bis Ende Oktober 2015) will grundlegende Fragen zur Ernährungsversorgung und zu den globalen Ressourcen und Herausforderungen mit den Hauptakteuren verhandeln. Dieses Thema soll am neuen Expo-Standort, einer ehemaligen Industriebrache im Nordwesten der Stadt, und wegen der Nachnutzung direkt neben dem neuen Messegelände von 2005 von Massimiliano Fuksas, in etwa 12 km Entfernung vom Zentrum Mailands platziert, auch städtebaulich demonstriert werden. Zwei senkrecht verlaufende Achsen werden, entsprechend der Anlage der antiken römischen Militärlager Cardo und Decumano genannt, das Gebiet gliedern, wobei die west-östliche Hauptachse Decumano wesentlich länger ausfällt als die nord-südliche Querachse Cardo. An dem mit Sonnensegeln verschatteten Decumano werden internationale Pavillons in verschiedenen Größen angesiedelt sein. Landwirtschaftliche Flächen, in Form von urbanen Gärten und in Clustern organisiert, werden Lebensmittel produzieren, und der Aushub für den großen See wird am Schlusspunkt des Cardo als Aussichtsberg dienen. Viele der sehr groß gedachten Expo-Projekte sind allerdings auf Probleme bei der Umsetzung gestoßen, sowohl inhaltlicher als auch infrastruktureller Natur. So wird beispielsweise die fünfte Metrolinie nicht pünktlich zur Expo fertig, sondern mit dem Bau wird erst nach der Expo begonnen. Im Vorfeld wurden etliche Skandale bezüglich der Korruption bei der Vergabe von Großaufträgen aufgedeckt. Man kennt ähnliche Geschichten aus der Vergangenheit und kann nur hoffen, dass es diesmal am Ende positiver für Mailand ausgehen wird.

Im Einklang mit den nachhaltigen Themen der Expo wurden parallel mehrere Stadtviertel Mailands umgebaut. Das wichtigste, weil zentralste und mit 340 000 Quadratmetern das größte, Konversionsprojekt Italiens stellt das neue Viertel Porta Nuova dar. Federführend ist der Projektentwickler Hines Italia, der seit etwas über zehn Jahren am Umbau dieses seit dem Krieg beschädigten und seit den 1970er-Jahren verwahrlosten Viertels in bester innerstädtischer Lage arbeitet. Das auch im Expo-Sinne auffälligste Teilprojekt ist Bosco Verticale, obwohl die beiden Türme mit ihren 112 und 80 Metern Höhe im Vergleich zu der aufstrebenden Skyline-Entwicklung niedrig sind. Denn das Zentrum des Viertels ist der mit 231 Metern derzeit höchste italienische Turm, der UniCredit Tower von

Moreover, the urban-development advantages such as the sparing use of space are convincing. As regards population density, each tower corresponds to a 50,000-square-metre area of single-family residential development, and in addition saves on potential commuter traffic. Within the context of urban planning, Porta Nuova represents a successful element in the general regeneration of Milan, and that after decades of economic decline, which was accompanied by a steep drop in the population from over 1.7 million in the 1970s to roughly 1.3 million today, as people moved away to the outskirts and new satellite towns. Urban planning development will culminate in Expo Milano 2015 with the slogan "Feeding the Planet. Energy for Life". The minds behind the Expo master plan are Ricky Burdett (from the London School of Economics), Jaques Herzog (from Basel-based architects Herzog & de Meuron) and Stefano Boeri. From May 1 to the end of October 2015, in discussions with the main protagonists, the Expo will address fundamental issues and challenges relating to food security and global resources. The town-planning implications of the topic are also to be demonstrated at the new Expo site, a former industrial wasteland in the northwest of the city, which, to ensure its use afterwards, is located right next to the new 2005 trade fair complex by Massimiliano Fuksas, some 12 km from central Milan. The site will be structured by two perpendicular axes named Cardo and Decumano after the layout of ancient Roman military camps; the main axis running from west to east, Decumano, will be considerably longer than the north-south axis Cardo. International pavilions of various sizes, shaded with awnings, will be situated along Decumano. Agricultural areas in the form of urban gardens organized in clusters will produce food, and the earth excavated to create the large lake will be heaped up to form a vantage point at the end of Cardo. However, many of the large-scale Expo projects have encountered problems both regarding the infrastructure and their execution. For example, the fifth metro line will not be finished in time for the Expo, but will only be begun afterwards. Countless scandals have been uncovered regarding corruption in the awarding of large contracts. We are familiar with such stories from the past and can only hope that this time things will turn out more positively for Milan.

In keeping with the sustainable topics of the Expo, several Milan districts have been redeveloped. Porta Nuova is the most central and largest district, covering 340,000 square metres, and represents Italy's largest conversion project. It is being overseen by project developer Hines Italia, which has been working on the district's redevelopment for over ten years. Though it enjoys a prime city location, it was damaged in the War and has been neglected since the 1970s. The Bosco Verticale project is the district's most striking element in relation to the Expo, although at just 112 and 80 metres tall the two buildings are relatively low compared to the towering skyline development. After all, the centre of the district is marked by what is currently Italy's tallest tower, the UniCredit Tower by Cesar Pelli, the new

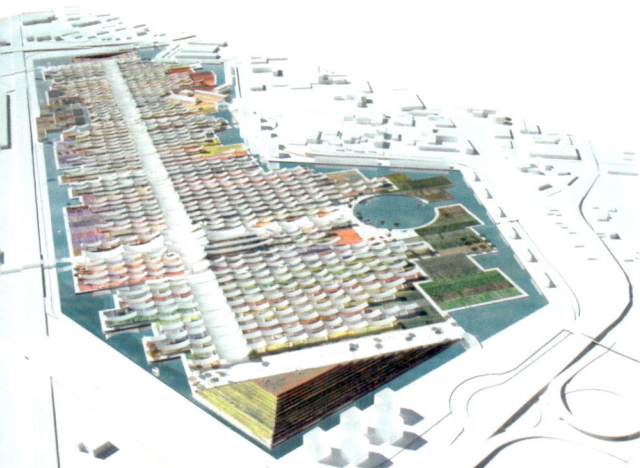

Der Blick vom Mailänder Dom auf die Skyline von Porta Nuova. Turm D des Bosco Verticale wird durch den UniCredit Tower verdeckt.
View of the skyline of Porta Nuova from the Milan Cathedral. Tower D of the Bosco Verticale is obscured by the UniCredit Tower.

Entwurf für das Gelände der Expo 2015 von den Architekten Herzog de Meuron aus Basel.
Design for the Expo 2015 site by Basel architecture firm Herzog de Meuron.

Stadtplan von Mailand mit Porta Nuova
City map of Milan with Porta Nuova

Cesar Pelli: die neue Zentrale der gleichnamigen Bank. Zu seinen Füßen ist ein überaus gelungener öffentlicher Platz entstanden, die Piazza Gae Aulenti, direkt über einem Eisenbahntunnel der Porta-Garibaldi-Station und einem Autotunnel gelegen, der die Hauptverkehrsanbindung aufrechterhält. Dieser intermodale Verkehrsknotenpunkt, der von gleich drei Metrolinien angefahren wird, sorgt für eine ständige Belebung des Platzes. Über neu geschaffene direkte Fußwege werden zudem bisher voneinander getrennte Stadtviertel verbunden. Direkt im Süden liegt die Innenstadt mit angesagten Adressen, wie 10 Corso Como, und sogar der Dom und die Galleria Vittorio Emmanuele sind mit etwa 2,5 Kilometern Entfernung immer noch zu Fuß zu erreichen. Im Norden liegt das frühere Arbeiterviertel Isola (isoliert, wie der Name Insel schon sagt) mit dem neuen 160 Meter hohen Verwaltungssitz der Region, dem Palazzo Lombardia von Pei Cobb Freed, und industriellen Lofts und Läden. Im Nordosten das Centro Direzionale der 1960er-Jahre mit seinen Verwaltungshochhäusern, darunter der ikonenhafte Grattacielo Pirelli von Gio Ponti, und im Osten das Viertel Varesine, das zur Piazza Repubblica mit ihren edlen Nobelhotels führt. Dort entstanden ebenfalls weitere Leuchtturmprojekte großer amerikanischer Architekturbüros, wie der gefaltete, 137 Meter hohe Diamond Tower und eine riesige unterirdische Mall von Kohn Pedersen Fox, sowie ein selbstbewusstes Wohnturmensemble von Arquitectonica mit 143 Metern Höhe. Etliche mittelhohe Wohn- und Bürobauten wurden von lokalen und von jüngeren Architekten (wie Cino Zucchi, Michele de Lucchi, M2P, Muñoz+Albin und Piuarch) gebaut, um die neuen Viertel mit den bestehenden Strukturen zu verweben. Sogar einige Kulturbauten hat der Projektentwickler errichtet – und betreibt sie fortan. Denn dort, wo der vertikale Wald heute steht, befand sich vor kurzem noch die leer stehende und von alternativen Kulturinitiativen besetzte ehemalige Fabrik „Stecca degli artigiani". Im neuen zweigeschossigen Kulturzentrum „L'Incubatore per l'Arte", ebenfalls von Stefano Boerri gebaut, sind deren frühere Nutzer heute mietfrei untergekommen.

Am meisten verwundert bei der Entstehung von Porta Nuova allerdings die Aufteilung der privaten und der öffentlichen Rollen: Der gesamte Städtebau und die begleitende Landschaftsplanung werden von einem privaten Developer finanziert und gesteuert und nicht, wie in Deutschland üblich, von einer öffentlichen Entwicklungsgesellschaft. Die Stadt Mailand hatte sich lediglich verpflichtet, den fast 90 000 Quadratmeter großen Park „I Giardini di Porta Nuova", geplant von Inside Outside aus Amsterdam, im Herzen des Gebiets zu errichten. Allerdings erst, nachdem der Developer das Gelände vorbereitet und einen Meter kontaminierten Bodens abgetragen und entsorgt hat. Dies ist bereits seit zwei Jahren abgeschlossen und seitdem hat sich hinter dem Bauzaun bedauerlicherweise nichts getan. Das zeitlich anvisierte Ziel Expo ist also nicht mehr zu schaffen. Es wäre zu wünschen, dass mit der steigenden internationalen Anerkennung für das Porta Nuova und besonders mit der Aufmerksamkeit für den, über die surreal leer geräumte Brache ragenden, Bosco Verticale eine Besinnung bei den Verantwortlichen eintritt.

headquarters of the eponymous bank. At its feet is an impressive public square, Piazza Gae Aulenti, located directly above a railway tunnel of the Porta Garibaldi station and a road tunnel that represents the primary traffic route. As this transit hub is used by three metro lines, the square is a constant buzz of activity. Moreover, districts that were previously separated from one another can now be reached on foot. Immediately to the south lies the inner city area with hip addresses such as 10 Corso Como, and it is even possible to walk to the cathedral and the Galleria Vittorio Emmanuele just 2.5 km away. In the north lies the onetime working-class area of Isola ('isolated' as its name 'island' suggests) with the new 160-metre-high administrative seat of the region, Palazzo Lombardia by Pei Cobb Freed, together with industrial lofts and shops. To the northeast is the Centro Direzionale, a 1960s' business district with its tall office blocks, including the iconic Grattacielo Pirelli by Gio Ponti, and in the east the Varesine district, which leads to Piazza Repubblica with its sophisticated upmarket hotels. Further landmark projects by major American architecture studios have also been created there, such as the 137-metre rhomboidal Diamond Tower by Kohn Pedersen Fox and an enormous underground mall, together with a self-confident residential tower ensemble by Arquitectonica rising up some 143 metres. A great many residential and office buildings of medium height have been built here by local and younger architects (such as Cino Zucchi, Michele de Lucchi, M2P, Muñoz+Albin and Piuarch), so as to blend the new district with the existing structures. The project developer even had several cultural buildings erected and continues to operate them. After all, until recently the location for the Vertical Forest was the site of the abandoned factory "Stecca degli artigiani", which was occupied by alternative cultural initiatives. The people who once operated it have been accommodated rent-free in the new two-storey cultural centre "L'Incubatore per l'Arte", also built by Stefano Boeri.

However, what is most surprising about the realization of Porta Nuova is the allocation of private and public roles: The entire urban development and the accompanying landscape planning are being financed and managed by a private developer and not, as is customary in Germany, by a public development firm. The city of Milan had undertaken only to realize the almost 90,000-square-metre park "I Giardini di Porta Nuova", planned by Inside Outside from Amsterdam, at the heart of the district – but only after the developer had prepared the area and removed and disposed of a metre of contaminated soil. Tragically, it is now two years since this was accomplished and nothing has happened behind the hoarding since then. The original deadline of the Expo is no longer feasible. It is to be hoped that as international recognition grows for Porta Nuova, and especially with the attention being grabbed by the Bosco Verticale, which looms over the surreal cleared wasteland, those responsible will come to their senses.

Der neue Quartiersplatz von Porta Nuova, die Piazza Gae Aulenti.
The new center of Porta Nuova, the Piazza Gae Aulenti.

Die Entwicklung des Porta-Nuova-Viertels in Mailand
Hines Italia SGR S.p.A.

Das Porta-Nuova-Projekt stellt sich der beachtlichen Herausforderung, einen heruntergekommenen – aber zentral gelegenen – Bereich Mailands zu sanieren. Drei Stadtviertel (Garibaldi, Varesine und Isola), die über 50 Jahre lang voneinander getrennt waren und nach der Stilllegung der bis in die 1960er-Jahre genutzten Eisenbahnlinien brach lagen, sollen dabei wieder miteinander verbunden und letztlich in das städtische Gefüge integriert werden. Bereits im 19. Jahrhundert, als sich der Mailänder Hauptbahnhof an der Piazza della Repubblica befand, führten die Eisenbahnverbindungen in Richtung Lombardei durch Garibaldi, Varesine und Isola. Als der Hauptbahnhof in den ersten Jahrzehnten des 20. Jahrhunderts an seinen derzeitigen Standort verlegt wurde, blieb in Varesine Platz für den Bahnhof Porta Nuova. Die Situation in diesem Viertel führte in den 1960er-Jahren zum Bau des Bahnhofs Porta Garibaldi, und so blieben die Planungen für dieses strategisch günstig gelegene Viertel über 40 Jahre in der Schwebe.

Der Immobilieninvestor Hines Italia SGR S.p.A. entwickelte sich zum Hauptbetreiber des wichtigsten Projekts in diesem Bezirk seit dem Zweiten Weltkrieg und begann, die wesentlichen Areale aufzukaufen (die bis dahin über 20 Grundstückseigentümern gehörten).

Es folgten Gespräche und Verhandlungen mit der Kommune, mit Vereinen und mit Bürgern, um ein Gesamtkonzept zu entwickeln, das die verschiedenen Bedürfnisse berücksichtigte: Das Porta-Nuova-Projekt ist somit Ergebnis der Zusammenarbeit vieler Beteiligter. Während aller Stadien der Projektentwicklung war diese Vorgehensweise ein zentrales Element für die Herangehensweise an diese für die Stadt einzigartige Chance: Im Verlauf des gesamten Prozesses bemühte sich Hines, die Auswirkungen der Bautätigkeiten so gering wie möglich zu halten, die Wünsche und Meinungen der Anwohner einzubeziehen und sie ständig auf dem Laufenden zu halten.

The development of the Porta Nuova district in Milan
Hines Italia SGR S.p.A.

Porta Nuova has taken up the challenge of redeveloping a degraded – but at the same central – area of Milan, by reconnecting and finally integrating three districts (Garibaldi, Varesine and Isola) that have been separated for over 50 years and partially abandoned after the dismantling of the railway infrastructure that had been operating until the 1960s. Already in the nineteenth century, when Milan's Central Station was in Piazza della Repubblica, the trains which served the Lombardy region used to cross the Garibaldi, Varesine and Isola areas. In the first decades of the twentieth century, when the Central Station was moved to its current location, it left room in Varesine for the Porta Nuova Station. In the 1960s, the Varesine situation led to the construction of the Porta Garibaldi Station, leaving projects for this strategic area hanging in the air for more than 40 years.

Hines Italia SGR became the promoter of one of the most significant projects within the area since the Second World War and started the procedures for purchasing the relevant areas (hitherto split into more than 20 properties).

This was followed by dialogues and negotiations with the city council, lobby groups and the city's inhabitants, in order to develop an overall project mindful of the various needs: Porta Nuova is therefore the result of joint work by many parties. This working method has been at the core of the approach to this important opportunity for the city during all stages of project development: Hines has always attempted to limit the impact of construction works, also taking into account the inhabitants' opinion and keeping them constantly updated.

Dank dieser Vorgehensweise entstand ein Projekt, das Wohn- und Gewerbeflächen, Büros, Begegnungsstätten, Kulturzentren, Ausstellungsräume und Dienstleistungsangebote umfasst und für Italien und Europa ein Vorbild in Bezug auf exzellente und nachhaltige Innovation unter Umwelt-, Bürgerbeteiligungs- und Infrastrukturaspekten darstellt. Die direkte Bürgerbeteiligung wird als neuer Weg zur Gestaltung einer urbanen Entwicklung verstanden, die von bestehenden Gebäuden und Strukturen ausgeht und die sozialen und ökologischen Bedürfnisse der Stadt berücksichtigt. Eine nachhaltige Infrastruktur ist insofern ein Ziel des Porta-Nuova-Projekts, da es eigene Fußgängerwege, unterirdische Straßen und Parkflächen zu einem effizienten Verkehrssystem kombiniert und zudem auf über 160 000 Quadratmetern Grünflächen, Plätze, Brücken und einen 90 000 Quadratmeter großen Park für Fußgänger und Radfahrer bieten soll. Ökologische Nachhaltigkeit strebt Hines durch eine Gestaltung des Viertels an, die die Umwelt respektiert und das Wohl der Menschen berücksichtigt. Aus diesem Grund unterwarf Hines das Projekt den strengen LEED-Standards (Leadership in Energy and Environmental Design), einem der renommiertesten internationalen Klassifizierungssystemen für ökologisches Bauen, und erhielt bei 30 Gebäuden die Vorzertifizierung und Zertifizierung LEED GOLD.

Der Porta-Nuova-Bezirk liegt an einem der Hauptverkehrsknotenpunkte Italiens: Er hat zwei Bahnhöfe, die eine Anbindung von Mailand nach Rom in weniger als drei Stunden und nach Paris in weniger als fünf Stunden möglich machen, sowie vier U-Bahnlinien und ein ausgedehntes oberirdisches Verkehrsnetz.

An dem Projekt sind diverse international renommierte sowie aufstrebende Architekten beteiligt, die sich in einem privaten Wettbewerb durchsetzen konnten: Cesar Pelli, KPF (Kohn Pederson Fox), Boeri Studio, Cucinella, Arquitectonica, Paolo Caputo, M2P Associati, Antonio Cittero Patricia Viel and Partners, Michele De Lucchi, Muñoz & Albin, Petra Blaisse, Andreas Kipar, Lucien Lagrange und Piuarch.

This approach has resulted in a project which includes properties to be used for residential and commercial purposes as well as offices, meeting places, cultural and exhibition centres and services, and which represents for Italy and Europe a model of excellence and sustainable innovation from an environmental, civic and infrastructural perspective. Civic sustainability is understood as a new way of shaping urban development, starting from the enhancement of existing buildings and structures and bearing in mind the social and environmental development needs of the city; infrastructural sustainability because the aim of the Porta Nuova project is to combine transportation efficiency with its own structure designed for pedestrians, building underground roads for cars, an underground parking system as well as a pedestrian and bicycle area of more than 160,000 square metres, with green areas, squares, bridges and a large park of 90,000 square metres; environmental sustainability because Hines' aim was to design an area which respected the environment and was mindful of people's well-being. This is why it submitted the project to the rigorous standards imposed by LEED, one of the most prestigious international systems for environmental certification, achieving the LEED GOLD pre-certification and certification for 30 buildings.

Porta Nuova is located in the country's main transport hub: two railway stations connecting Milan to Rome in less than three hours and to Paris in less than five hours, four subway lines and an extensive surface transport network.

Various internationally renowned and up-and-coming architects have taken part in the project, through private competitions: Cesar Pelli, KPF (Kohn Pederson Fox), Boeri Studio, Cucinella, Arquitectonica, Paolo Caputo, M2P Associati, Antonio Citterio Patricia Viel and Partners, Michele De Lucchi, Muñoz + Albin, Petra Blaisse, Andreas Kipar, Lucien Lagrange and Piuarch.

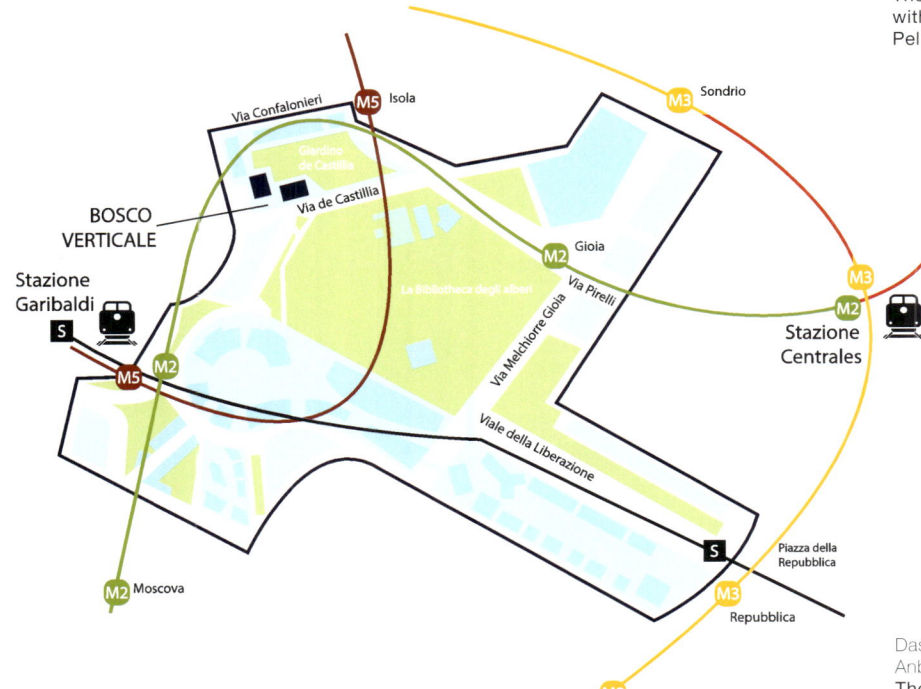

Die Skyline des neu entwickelten Viertels Porta Nuova mit Hochhäusern von Kohn Pedersen Fox, Arquitectonica, Pelli Clarke Pelli, Boeri Studio u.a.
The skyline of the newly developed district of Porta Nuova with skyscrapers by Kohn Pedersen Fox, Arquitectonica, Pelli Clarke Pelli, Boeri Studio and others

Das neue Stadtquartier verfügt über eine erstklassige Anbindung an den öffentlichen Nah- und Fernverkehr.
The new city district has excellent connections to local and long-distance public transport.

Das Grün des Bosco Verticale

Laura Gatti, Studio Laura Gatti, Grünplanerin Bosco Verticale, Mailand

Der Bosco Verticale, der „vertikale Wald", ist „ein Experiment für das Zusammenleben von Bäumen und Menschen" (Stefano Boeri). Er dient als Modell für ein nachhaltiges Wohngebäude und trägt als Begrünungsprojekt in Metropolen zur Regeneration der Umwelt und zur urbanen Biodiversität bei.

Die Vegetation des Bosco Verticale ist so dicht gestaltet, dass sie die äußere Fassadenschicht bildet. Dank der dichten und homogenen Bepflanzung präsentiert sich die äußere Hülle als „Mineralwand" oder „grünes Kleid" der Hochhäuser, bildet einen Filter zwischen Innen und Außen. Zugleich sorgt sie für das auffallende Erscheinungsbild der Bauten.

Jede Fassade und jedes Stockwerk weist je nach Anforderungen der verschiedenen Arten und abhängig von den mikroklimatischen Bedingungen ein anderes Pflanzschema auf. So entstehen letztlich über 400 Gärten unterschiedlicher Größe und Pflanzenzusammenstellung. Zudem sind die Pflanzen so ausgewählt, dass sie für ein angenehmes Klima in den Wohnungen sorgen: immergrüne an der Süd- und Westseite, laubabwerfende an der Nord- und Ostseite.

Die Pflanzengruppen sind nach Farbe und Blütezeit zusammengestellt. Farbwechsel ergeben sich in drei der vier Jahreszeiten: im Frühjahr, im Sommer und im Herbst. Einige duftende Blüten sorgen für ein unmittelbares Naturerlebnis. Im Herbst sorgen die warmen Farben des Laubes und der Rinde und im Winter winterblühende Pflanzen für ein attraktives Erscheinungsbild.

Das Ensemble hängender Gärten, das eine Grünfläche von 12 000 Quadratmetern erreicht, umfasst:
– 94 verschiedene Pflanzenarten;
– 60 verschiedene Baum- und Straucharten (mehr als gemeinhin in einem öffentlichen Park von 5000 bis 6000 Quadratmetern);
– 66 nützliche Arten für Bestäuber;
– 59 nützliche Arten für Vögel (Nahrung, Nistplätze);
– 62 attraktive Arten für Schmetterlinge;
– 33 immergrüne Arten, die Wildtieren selbst im Winter Schutz und Nahrung bieten und den Bosco Verticale zu einem Biodiversitäts-Hotspot in der Stadt machen.

Am Anfang der Planung standen verschiedene Untersuchungen zur Nachhaltigkeit des Projekts: Mikrometeorologische Studien stellten den Wasserbedarf und die Auswirkungen der Höhe auf die normalen Vegetationszyklen fest; Schätzungen zur Dauer der Sonneneinstrahlung und des Schattens halfen, eine ausgewogene Bepflanzung zu konzipieren; die CO_2-Aufnahme, die Senkung der Fassadentemperatur und die Feinstaubreduzierung wurden auf jährlicher Basis berechnet.

Es gab ausführliche Diskussionen über die angemessene Größe der Pflanzcontainer, um hinsichtlich der Nährstoff- und Wasserversorgung, vor allem aber unter mechanischen Stabilitätsaspekten der Bäume ein adäquates Wachstum zu gewährleisten. So werden die Bäume in einen Kubikmeter Substrat gepflanzt, wobei

The Green of Bosco Verticale

Laura Gatti, Studio Laura Gatti, Botanical consultant Bosco Verticale, Milan

Bosco Verticale is "an experiment of cohabitation between trees and people" (Stefano Boeri). It is a model for a sustainable residential building and a project for the metropolitan reforestation that contributes to the regeneration of the environment and urban biodiversity.

The vegetation of Bosco Verticale has been designed to be incredibly dense in order to function as the outermost layer of the façade itself. The primary enclosure of the "mineral wall" shows this "green dress" of the towers, due to the density and homogeneity of the planting, and represents a filter between the inside and the outside, creating a striking image of the building.

Each façade, and every floor, shows a different planting scheme, varying according to the needs of the different species and the microclimatic conditions. The final result is more than 400 gardens differing by size and species assortment. The plantings have been also designed to ensure comfort in the flats themselves, putting evergreens on the south and west sides, and deciduous trees on the north and east sides.

The plant groups were divided by colour and flowering time. Colour changes are related to three seasons: spring, summer and autumn. Scented blooms help to keep alive the sense of nature. In autumn the attraction is ensured by the warm colours of the foliage and of the barks, while the ornamental effect in winter is ensured by the presence of plants that bloom in this season.

In a system of hanging gardens that could reach a green surface of 12,000 square metres, you can find:
– 94 different plant species
– 60 different species of trees and shrubs (more than commonly found in a neighbourhood public park of 5-6,000 square metres)
– 66 useful species for pollinators
– 59 useful species for birds (food, nesting)
– 62 species attractive to butterflies
– 33 evergreen species that provide shelter and food for wildlife even in winter, making the Bosco Verticale a hotspot for biodiversity in the city.

At the beginning of the design process, different studies have been carried out to investigate the sustainability of the project: micrometeorological studies have been made to identify needs in term of water and impact of the elevation on the normal vegetation cycles; sun exposure and shadow duration were evaluated to understand how plantings could be balanced; the CO_2 uptake benefit, façade temperature decrease and PM10 removal were calculated on an annual basis.

A lengthy discussion was held to identify the proper size of the containers to guarantee adequate growth not only in terms of nutrients and available water requirements but, above all, of the mechanical stability of trees.

Herbst **Autumn** (HA)

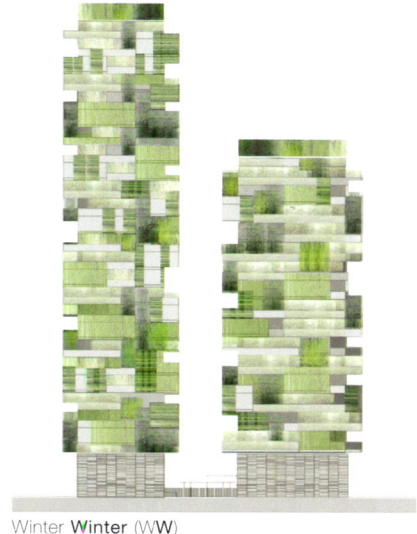

Winter **Winter** (WW)

Rotbuche
Common beech

Felsenbirne „Robin Hill"
Juneberry Camellia "Robin Hill"

Perückenstrauch
Purple smoke bush

Kamelie
Camellia

HA   WW   FS   SS

Baum-Hasel
Turkish hazel

Zierapfel "Red Jewel"
Crabapple

Westl. Erdbeerbaum
Strawberry tree

Purpur-Weide
Purple osier

HA   WW   FS   SS

Das wechselnde Erscheinungsbild der Türme am Beispiel der Westfassade. Die Bepflanzung der einzelnen Fassaden orientiert sich stark an den verschiedenen Himmelsrichtungen und den daraus resultierenden Witterungseinflüssen und variiert nach Höhe des Gebäudes.

This example of the western façade illustrates the changing appearance of the towers. The plantings on the individual façades are strongly oriented toward the different directions of the compass and the associated weather conditions, and they vary according to the height of the building.

Frühling **Spring** (FS)

Sommer **Summer** (SS)

Gold-Gleditsche
Honey locust

Schneekirsche
Spring cherry

Stern-Magnolie
Star magnolia

Primel-Jasmin
Primerose jasmine

HA   WW   FS   SS

Steineiche
Evergreen oak

Wilde Olive
Wild Olive

Granatapfel
Pomegranate

Ähriger Lilienrasen
Creeping lily turf

HA   WW   FS   SS

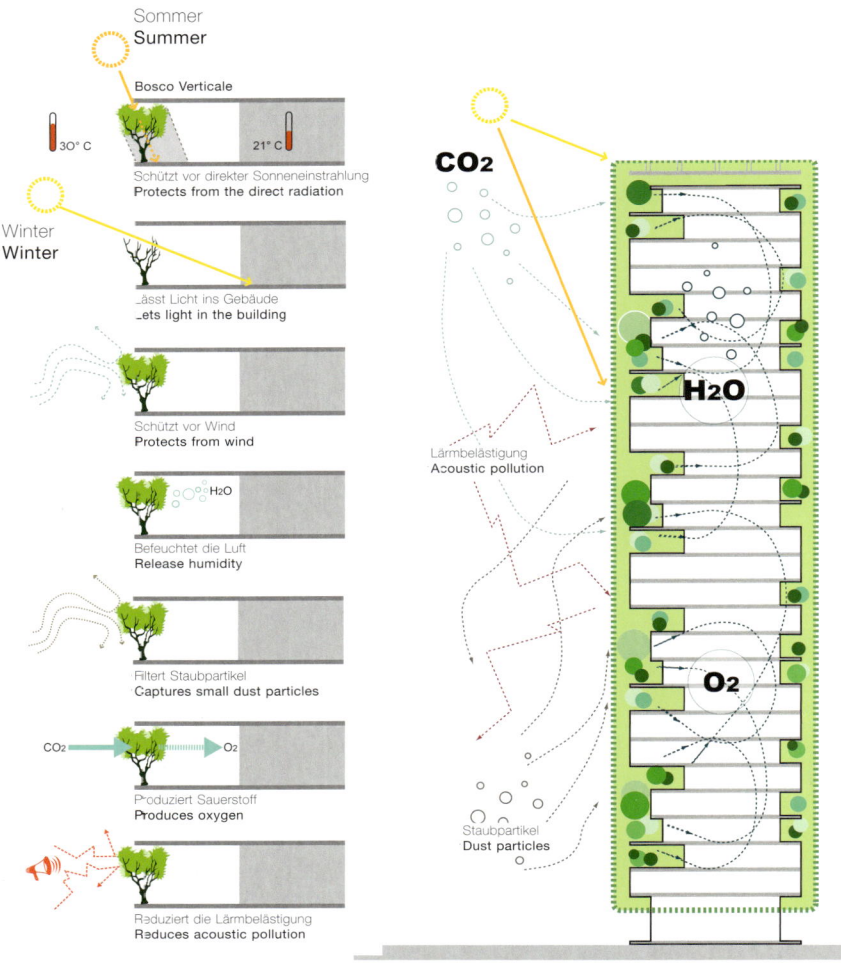

Sommer
Summer

Bosco Verticale

30° C   21° C

Schützt vor direkter Sonneneinstrahlung
Protects from the direct radiation

Winter
Winter

Lässt Licht ins Gebäude
Lets light in the building

Schützt vor Wind
Protects from wind

H_2O

Befeuchtet die Luft
Release humidity

Filtert Staubpartikel
Captures small dust particles

CO_2 O_2

Produziert Sauerstoff
Produces oxygen

Reduziert die Lärmbelästigung
Reduces acoustic pollution

CO_2

H_2O

O_2

Lärmbelästigung
Acoustic pollution

Staubpartikel
Dust particles

Die Vorzüge der begrünten Fassade ersetzen moderne Klimatechnik
The advantages of the green façades supersede modern air-conditioning technology.

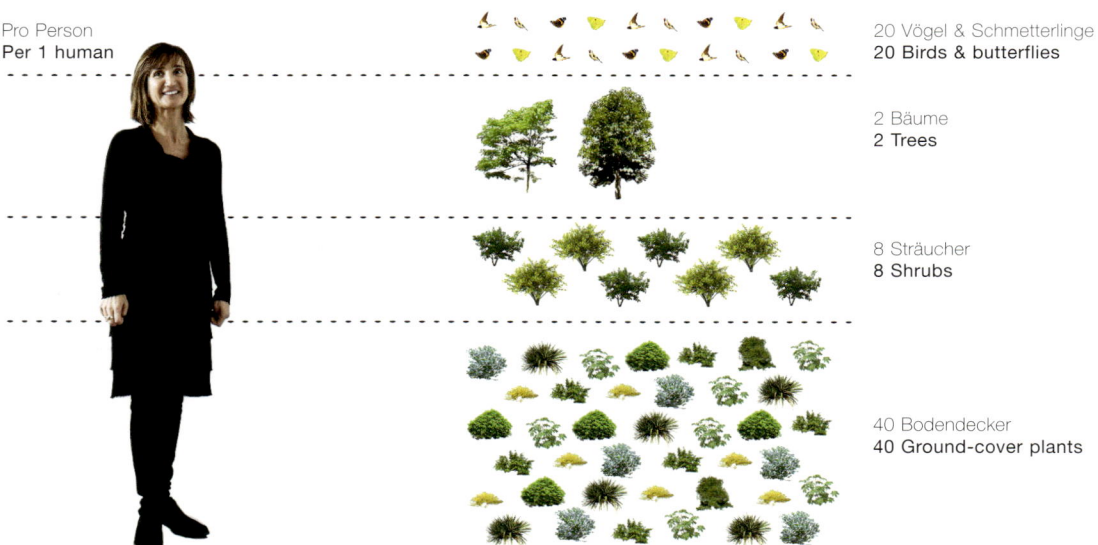

Pro Person
Per 1 human

20 Vögel & Schmetterlinge
20 Birds & butterflies

2 Bäume
2 Trees

8 Sträucher
8 Shrubs

40 Bodendecker
40 Ground-cover plants

Die Aufforstung am Bosco Verticale am Beispiel eines einzelnen Bewohners
Forestation on the Bosco Verticale illustrated through a single resident

die Breite und Länge der Behälter je nach Baumgröße zur besseren Lastverteilung variiert. Ein Metallgitter am Behälterboden dient den Wurzelballen als Verankerung.

Das Pflanzsubstrat wurde eigens entwickelt, getestet und später aus einer Mischung von Mutterboden, unterschiedlichen Anteilen organischer Zusätze je nach Substrattiefe und leichten Bimssteinen verschiedener Größe zusammengestellt.

Da an den Gebäuden mit hohen Windgeschwindigkeiten zu rechnen ist, wurden die möglichen Auswirkungen auf die Bäume im Windkanal getestet. Diese Versuche brachten zudem Aufschluss darüber, welche Gebäudeseiten und Stockwerke den größten Windlasten ausgesetzt sind: Für diese Bereiche wurden die Bäume besonders sorgfältig ausgewählt und zusätzlich zu dem Wurzelballenanker und den oberirdischen Halterungen gegen Windbruch mit einer dritten Verankerung in Form eines unterirdischen Metallrahmens versehen.

Aus dem vorläufigen Konzept des „Baumsystems" ergaben sich somit eine Reihe Maßvorgaben und äußere Parameter: a) Baumart, Baumhöhe, Stammdicke, Kronengröße, geschätzter Strömungswiderstandskoeffizient; b) Containergröße, Substrat mit festgelegten geotechnischen Eigenschaften; c) Verankerung – im Boden und in der Luft. Die Lösung, die sich nach den ersten Studien als die beste empfahl, wurde weiter getestet, indem die Bäume Windgeschwindigkeiten bis zu 190 Stundenkilometern ausgesetzt wurden. Die Ergebnisse bestätigten die Annahmen, die der beratende Landschaftsarchitekt über die geplante Dimensionierung der Bäume prognostiziert hatte, und halfen, die Dimensionen des oberirdischen Haltesystems final festzulegen.

Anschließend wurden die Bäume in das belüftete Substrat gepflanzt und beschnitten, um in einer zweijährigen Vorkulturperiode etwaige Strukturdefekte korrigieren zu können und die Krone auf die richtige Größe zu bringen.

Nach den Verdunstungsberechnungen beträgt der gesamte Wasserbedarf für die Begrünung des kleineren Towers 2370 Kubikmeter und für die des höheren 4450 Kubikmeter pro Jahr. Das begrünte Dach recycelt das Brauchwasser des Gebäudes (unter anderem aus der mit Grundwasser gespeisten Klimaanlage) und ist somit überaus nachhaltig. Das Bewässerungssystem ist auf den Wasserbedarf sowie auf die Verteilung der Pflanzen auf die Stockwerke und auf ihren Standort abgestimmt. Sensoren erfassen die jeweilige Feuchtigkeit und schalten die Bewässerung ein und aus.

Die Sicherheit hatte bei der Planung des Bosco Verticale Priorität und war auch ein Hauptanliegen bei der Wartung. Mehrere Aspekte wurden berücksichtigt, um maximale Sicherheit für die Pflanzen zu gewährleisten:

– Ein Kriterium bei der Auswahl der Pflanzen war ihre Anpassungsfähigkeit an die Witterungsverhältnisse.
– Die Vorkultur in Containern war auf die Entwicklung bestens angepasster Wurzeln und besonders widerstandsfähiger Pflanzen ausgerichtet.

Trees are planted in one metre of substrate, and to optimize the loads, width and length are variable depending on the size of the specimen. At the bottom, a metal grid provides for the attachment of the root ball's anchoring system.

The growing medium has been designed, tested and later prepared starting from a mix of natural soil, organic compounds in different percentages depending on the depth of the substrate and light lava rocks (pumice stones) of different sizes.

Because of the high wind speeds expected on-site, early evaluations in a wind tunnel were carried out to show how wind could affect trees; secondly, a wind-tunnel test helped to identify the side and the height of the most exposed locations: trees in these positions were carefully selected, and a third anchorage system (an underground metal frame) was arranged in addition to the root-ball anchor system and the anti-breakage aerial system.

As a result, the preliminary design of the "tree-system" led to a set of measurements and physical parameters: a) tree species, tree height, trunk size, crown area, estimated drag coefficient; b) container size, soil with defined geotechnical properties; c) anchor systems, both aerial and underground. The solution that seemed best, based on the preliminary studies, was further tested on trees with wind speeds up to 190 km/h. Results confirmed the assumptions of the preliminary dimensioning of the trees made by the landscape consultant, and helped to establish the final dimension of the aerial safety system.

After that the trees were placed in the aerated substrate, and pruned to correct any structural defects and to shape the crown at the correct size during a period of pre-cultivation lasting two years.

A transpiration model estimates that the total annual water requirement for the smaller tower is 2,370 cubic metres and for the taller tower 4,450 cubic metres per year. The green roof system recycles the water resulting from other and different uses (air-conditioning systems with the use of ground water), and therefore is highly sustainable. The irrigation system has been designed with a view to the water needs and the distribution of plants across floors and their positions. Sensors detect the humidity conditions and activate and stop irrigation as required.

Safety was a priority during the design process of Bosco Verticale, and is still the main goal of maintenance works. Several elements have been studied to guarantee maximum safety for the plants:

– the choice of plants was made taking account of their ability to adapt to weather conditions;
– the pre-growing stage in containers was designed to produce perfectly adapted roots and particularly hardy plants;
– the containers which host the plants are fitted with special systems to avoid movement or lifting up of the root balls;

– Die Pflanzgefäße sind mit Spezialsystemen ausgestattet, die ein Verlagern oder das Anheben der Wurzelballen verhindern.
– Für größere Bäume wurden Halterungen entwickelt, die eine zusätzliche Verankerung sowie Flexibilität gewährleisten und sich an das Wachstum ces Baumes anpassen.
– Sämtliche Sicherheitsvorkehrungen unterliegen im Rahmen der jährlichen Wartung regelmäßigen Kontrollen.

Zwei Jahre nachdem der erste Baum gepflanzt wurde, steht fest, dass der Bosco Verticale die Schaffung eines urbaner Ökosystems fördert, da seine verschiedenen Grünflächen (kürzlich ergänzt um zwei speziell auf Artenvielfalt ausgerichtete begrünte Dächer) von wild lebenden Arten besiedelt werden: von Solitärbienen, Hummeln, Marienkäfern bis hin zu verschiedenen Vogelarten.

So entwickelt sich der Bosco Verticale zum Anziehungspunkt und zum Symbol für die Wiederbesiedelung der Stadt durch Pflanzen und Tiere.

– a holding system was designed for the larger trees to provide extra anchoring and flexibility while being capable of adapting to the growth of the tree;
– all safety measures are subject to regular inspections as part of the annual maintenance program.

After two years from the first tree planting, it is clear that the Bosco Verticale enhances the establishment of an urban ecosystem, in which its various green systems (with the recent addition of two green roofs specially designed for biodiversity) are being colonized by wildlife species such as solitary bees, bumblebees, ladybirds and different species of birds.

The Bosco Verticale is becoming both a magnet for, and a symbol of, the re-colonization of the city by vegetation and animal life.

Sowohl in als auch über der Erde sind die Bäume gegen die wirkenden Windlasten geschützt.
Trees are protected from wind forces both above and below the soil.

Besichtigung Bosco Verticale in Mailand, Juni 2014
Visiting Bosco Verticale in Milan, June 2014

Von links nach rechts **Left to right**: Claudio Saibene
(Bauleitung **Construction Director**, Hines Italia), Peter Cachola
Schmal (Direktor **Director**, Deutsches Architekturmuseum),
Silke Schuster-Muller (Leiterin Gesellschaftliches Engagement
Head of Social Concerns, DekaBank), Marika Beuthan
(Presse **Press Office**, DekaBank)

Von links nach rechts **Left to right**: Davor Popovic
(Projektleiter **Executive architect** Bosco Verticale, Boeri
Studio), Stefano Boeri und and Laura Gatti (Grünplanerin
Botanical consultant Bosco Verticale)

Besichtigung der Gebäude mit Planern und Ingenieuren
Tour of the building with planners and engineers

Die Fotos für den Internationalen Hochhaus Preis machte vor
Ort die Fotografin Kirsten Bucher
**The photos for the International Highrise Award were taken
on site by Kirsten Bucher.**

Im Gespräch mit Manfredi Catella, Geschäftsführer Hines Italia
Meeting with Manfredi Catella, CEO of Hines Italia

Peter Cachola Schmal im Gespräch mit Stefano Boeri, dahinter
Peter Körner (Koordinator/Kurator IHP 2014, Deutsches
Architekturmuseum)
**Peter Cachola Schmal in discussion with Stefano Boeri,
Peter Körner (coordinator/curator IHA 2014, Deutsches
Architekturmuseum) pictured behind**

Inhalt **Contents**

Vorwort

Prof. Dr. Felix Semmelroth
Dezernent für Kultur und Wirtschaft der Stadt Frankfurt
am Main

Dr. Matthias Danne
Mitglied des Vorstands der DekaBank

Peter Cachola Schmal
Direktor des Deutschen Architekturmuseums

In Verbindung mit der Verleihung und der Ausstellung
zum Internationalen Hochhaus Preis publiziert das
Deutsche Architekturmuseum alle zwei Jahre einen
Katalog, den die DekaBank finanziert. In diesem Jahr
wurden 26 Projekte aus 17 Ländern für die Auszeichnung nominiert, die hier detailliert vorgestellt
werden. Anhand dieser Auswahl werden die globalen
Trends der aktuellen Hochhausarchitektur aufgezeigt
und beleuchtet.

Nachdem die ersten beiden Preisträger, 2004 De
Hoftoren in Den Haag von Kohn Pedersen Fox (London)
und 2006 der Torre Agbar von den Pariser Architekten
Ateliers Jean Nouvel in Barcelona, aus Europa kamen,
wurden in den folgenden Jahren Hochhäuser auf
diversen anderen Kontinenten ausgezeichnet: in
Nordamerika 2008 die Hearst Headquarters in New
York von Foster + Partners aus London, in Asien 2010
The Met in Bangkok von WOHA Architects aus
Singapur und 2012 in Australien 1 Bligh Street in
Sydney von ingenhoven architects aus Düsseldorf in
Zusammenarbeit mit dem australischen Büro
Architectus. In diesem Jahr wird der Preis wieder an
ein europäisches Projekt vergeben. Die Jury entschied
sich für das Projekt „Bosco Verticale" in Mailand von
Boeri Studio, ebenfalls aus Mailand. Die beiden
verhältnismäßig kleinen Wohntürme sind Teil einer
umfangreichen Quartiersentwicklung im Mailänder
Norden. Gemeinsam mit einem weitläufigen Park bilden
sie das grüne Herzstück des neu entwickelten Viertels,
das weitere Hochhäuser und Großbauten umfasst.
Durch die vertikale Fortführung der Parkfläche auf den
122 und 75 Meter hohen Türmen werden mitten in der
Stadt Bäume und Pflanzen eingesetzt, die sonst eine
zusätzliche Fläche von 5000 bis 6000 Quadratmetern
benötigen würden. Somit sind die beiden Türme

Preface

Prof Dr Felix Semmelroth
Deputy Mayor in Charge of Culture and Science of
the City of Frankfurt

Dr Matthias Danne
Member of the Management Board, DekaBank

Peter Cachola Schmal
Director, Deutsches Architekturmuseum

In connection with the bestowal of the International
Highrise Award and the associated exhibition,
every two years the Deutsches Architekturmuseum
publishes a catalogue which is financed by the
DekaBank. This year, 26 projects from 17 countries
were nominated for the award; they are presented
here in detail. Using this selection, global trends in
current highrise architecture are illustrated and
highlighted.

After the first two recipients came from Europe –
De Hoftoren in The Hague by Kohn Pederson Fox
(London) in 2004 and the Torre Agbar in Barcelona
by the Paris-based architects Ateliers Jean Nouvel
in 2006 – the following years saw highrises on
several other continents win the award: the Hearst
Headquarters in New York, North America, by
Foster + Partners from London in 2008, The Met in
Bangkok, Asia, by WOHA Architects from
Singapore in 2010 and 1 Blight Street in Sydney,
Australia, by ingenhoven architects from Düsseldorf
in collaboration with the Australian architectural
firm Architectus in 2012. This year the award goes
to a European project again. The jury chose the
project "Bosco Verticale" in Milan, designed by
Boeri Studio, also based in Milan. The two
comparatively small residential towers are part of a
comprehensive development of the quarter in the
north of the city. Together with extensive parklands
they form the green core of the newly developed
neighbourhood, which contains further highrises
and large buildings. As a result of the vertical
continuation of the park area into the two towers,
122 m and 75 m tall respectively, trees and plants
have been deployed in the middle of the city that
would otherwise require an additional space of

Jurysitzung des Internationalen Hochhaus Preises 2014 in der DekaBank, Frankfurt am Main
Jury session of the International Highrise Award 2014 at DekaBank, Frankfurt am Main

einzigartige Prototypen für ein grünes, nachhaltiges Wohnen in einer dicht besiedelten Stadt wie Mailand. Jede der 400 Wohnungen verfügt über mindestens einen begrünten, großflächigen Balkon. Deren Vegetation sorgt für eine natürliche Klimatisierung der Wohnungen und bietet den Bewohnern eine außergewöhnliche Aufenthaltsqualität. Die Pionierarbeit, die für die Bepflanzung einer Hochhausfassade in Europa notwendig war, beschreibt die Grünplanerin Laura Gatti in einem ausführlichen Essay.

Der Preisträger ging auch in diesem Jahr aus einem Kreis von fünf Finalisten hervor.

In ihrem Inneren umschließt die skulpturale Hochhausgruppe Sliced Porosity Block – Raffles City Chengdu von Steven Holl Architects aus New York einen von Lärm und Verkehr abgeschotteten Platz. Zugleich ist dieser über mehrere Zugänge mit der umliegenden Stadt verbunden und so nicht nur für die Bewohner der fünf Hochhäuser erreichbar. Das Ensemble und der detailreich geplante öffentliche Raum sind ein richtungsweisendes Beispiel für Hochhausbau und Stadtplanung in dicht besiedelten Megacities.

Mit One Central Park in Sydney und dem Renaissance Barcelona Fira Hotel in Barcelona sind gleich zwei Projekte von Jean Nouvel unter den Finalisten. One Central Park ist ein „Mixed-Use"-Projekt, bestehend aus zwei unterschiedlich hohen Türmen, die über einen gemeinsamen Sockel miteinander verbunden sind. Der Zwischenraum der ebenfalls begrünten Türme wird durch die Umleitung von Tageslicht natürlich belichtet. Das Projekt zeigt, wie erfolgreiche Nachverdichtung in einer Metropole wie Sydney möglich ist.

Das Renaissance Barcelona Fira Hotel besteht aus zwei parallelen Hochhausscheiben, in denen die Hotelzimmer untergebracht sind. Dazwischen befinden sich die Verkehrswege und öffentlichen Bereiche in einem offenen Zwischenraum, durchflutet vom mediterranen Klima und gesäumt von üppiger Begrünung. Auf diese Art erlebt der Besucher eindrucksvoll die Interaktion von Innen und Außen sowie Technik und Natur.

De Rotterdam vom Office for Metropolitan Architecture vereint diverse Nutzungen geschichtet und vernetzt in

5000 to 6000 square metres. The two towers are therefore unique prototypes of green, sustainable living in a densely populated city such as Milan. Each one of the 400 flats possesses at least one large balcony lavishly covered in plants. This vegetation is a natural air-conditioning system for the flats, and offers the residents exceptionally high-quality space to spend their time. Greenspace architect Laura Gatti describes in a detailed essay the pioneering work that was necessary for planting plants on a highrise façade in Europe.

Once again the award winners emerged from a group of five finalists.

In its interior, the sculptural highrise complex Sliced Porosity Block – Raffles City Chengdu by Steven Holl Architects in New York encloses a space shielded from noise and traffic. At the same time it is connected to the surrounding city via several access points, thereby also making it accessible to non-residents of the five highrises. The ensemble and the public space, which has undergone detailed planning, are a seminal example of highrise construction and town planning in densely populated megacities.

Jean Nouvel has two projects among the finalists, namely One Central Park in Sydney and the Renaissance Barcelona Fira Hotel in Barcelona. One Central Park is a "mixed-use" project, consisting of two towers of different heights that are connected to each other via a shared base. The space between the towers, which are also covered in plants, is lit naturally by channelling daylight. The project shows how successful densification is possible in a city like Sydney.

The Renaissance Barcelona Fira Hotel consists of two parallel highrise blocks in which the hotel rooms are housed. Between them are transport routes and public areas in an open space, flooded by a Mediterranean climate and lined by lavish vegetation. Visitors are given an impressive demonstration of the interaction between the interior and exterior as well as between technology and nature.

einem einzigen Gebäude. Diese experimentelle Weiterentwicklung des modernen Hochhauses gleicht einer vertikalen Stadt in der extremen Formensprache des Rotterdamers Rem Koolhaas.

Nach der gemeinsamen Initiierung 2003 durch die Stadt Frankfurt am Main, das Deutsche Architekturmuseum und die DekaBank wurde der Internationale Hochhaus Preis erstmals im Jahr 2004 offiziell vergeben. Seitdem wird er alle zwei Jahre in partnerschaftlicher Kooperation organisiert sowie finanziert. Somit feiert der Preis in diesem Jahr bei seiner sechsten Verleihung sein 10-jähriges Jubiläum.

In der Stadt Frankfurt am Main verfügt der Hochhausbau über eine gewisse Tradition. Die seit dem Zweiten Weltkrieg wachsende Skyline war über Jahrzehnte nicht nur singulär in Deutschland, sondern auch richtungsweisend für Europa. Anhand der gebauten Hochhäuser definierte sich Frankfurt am Main stets aufs Neue als selbstbewusste Metropole. Mit dem Engagement für den Internationalen Hochhaus Preis möchte die Stadt Frankfurt am Main aufzeigen, dass im Hochhausbau nicht allein die Höhenmeter, sondern vielmehr zukunftsweisende Gesamtkonzepte in Bezug auf Nachhaltigkeit und Wirtschaftlichkeit, Einbindung in den urbanen Kontext, Design und Technik sowie Aufenthaltsqualität maßgebend sind. Somit richtet sich der Internationale Hochhaus Preis an innovative Bauten mit einer Mindesthöhe von 100 Metern, die herausragende Beiträge zur Entwicklung der internationalen Hochhausarchitektur darstellen.

Der Internationale Hochhaus Preis ist 2014 zum sechsten Mal wichtiger Bestandteil des umfangreichen gesellschaftlichen Engagements der DekaBank. Das Institut ist Teil der Sparkassen-Finanzgruppe, die mit einer Summe von 150 Millionen Euro jährlich größter nichtstaatlicher Kulturförderer Deutschlands ist.

Die DekaBank ist das Wertpapierhaus der Sparkassen und einer der größten Anbieter von Offenen Immobilienfonds in Deutschland. Gemeinsam mit ihren Tochtergesellschaften bildet sie die Deka-Gruppe. Das Geschäftsfeld Immobilien bündelt die Immobilienkompetenz der Gruppe. Die Kapitalanlagegesellschaften Deka Immobilien Investment GmbH und WestInvest Gesellschaft für Investmentfonds mbH sind

De Rotterdam by the Office for Metropolitan Architecture combines various uses layered and linked in a single building. This experimental development of the modern highrise resembles a vertical city in the extreme language of forms used by Rotterdam architect Rem Koolhaas.

After the joint initiation by the city of Frankfurt am Main, the Deutsches Architekturmuseum and DekaBank in 2003, the International Highrise Award was officially presented for the first time in 2004. Ever since then it has been organized and funded every two years in a co-operative partnership. Thus this year, when the award will be made for the sixth time, it will also enjoy its tenth anniversary.

Highrise construction has a certain tradition in Frankfurt. The skyline, which has been growing since the Second World War, was unique in Germany for decades and also seminal for Europe. Frankfurt constantly redefined itself as a self-confident city through the highrises being built there. With its commitment to the International Highrise Award, the city of Frankfurt wants to demonstrate that it is not just height that matters in highrise construction; instead, forward-looking concepts focusing on sustainability and economic viability, integration into the urban context, design, technology and on the quality of experience the building provides people with are all key. The International Highrise Award therefore looks at innovative structures with a minimum height of 100 metres that have made outstanding contributions to the development of international highrise architecture.

For the sixth time now, the International Highrise Award is an important part of DekaBank's comprehensive corporate commitment. The institute is a member of the Sparkassen-Finanzgruppe, which is the biggest non-governmental patron of culture in Germany, donating a sum of 150 million euros annually.

DekaBank is the investment management institution for the Sparkasse banks and one of the largest providers of open-end real-estate funds in Germany. Together with its subsidiaries it forms the

Jurysitzung des Internationalen Hochhaus Preises 2014 in der DekaBank, Frankfurt am Main
Jury session of the International Highrise Award 2014 at DekaBank, Frankfurt am Main

Juroren des Internationalen Hochhaus Preises 2014 **Jurors of the International Highrise Award 2014**
Von links nach rechts **From left to right**: Louisa Hutton, Sauerbruch Hutton, Berlin; Jan Knippers, Professor für Tragkonstruktionen und Konstruktives Entwerfen **Professor of Building Structures and Structural Design**, Universität Stuttgart; Yew-Thong Leong, Professor für Architektur **Professor of architecture, Ryerson University, Toronto**; Horst R. Muth, Leiter Projektmanagement Immobilien **Head of real estate management**, Deka Immobilien GmbH, Frankfurt am Main; Swantje Kühn, GKK+Architekten, Berlin; Christoph Ingenhoven, ingenhoven architects, Juryvorsitz **Chairman of the jury**, Düsseldorf; Peter Cachola Schmal, Direktor **Director** Deutsches Architekturmuseum, Frankfurt am Main; Neil Thomas, atelier one, London
Nicht auf dem Foto **Missing on the picture**: Thomas Schmengler, Geschäftsführer **Managing director of** Deka Immobilien GmbH, Frankfurt am Main; Prof. Dr. Felix Semmelroth, Dezernent für Kultur und Wirtschaft der Stadt Frankfurt am Main **Deputy Mayor in Charge of Culture and Science of the City of Frankfurt**

große Investoren auf den gewerblichen europäischen Immobilienmärkten. Mehr als 450 Objekte in 23 Ländern gehören zum Bestand der Immobilienfonds. Eine nachhaltige Geschäftsausrichtung, sowohl in ökologischer als auch in ökonomischer Hinsicht, sieht die Deka-Gruppe in ihrer Eigenschaft als Wertpapierhaus der Sparkassen-Finanzgruppe in ihrer Verantwortung. Neben der zentralen Investitionsmaxime der Wirtschaftlichkeit stellt Nachhaltigkeit ein bedeutendes Kriterium dar, an dem auch die zum Internationalen Hochhaus Preis nominierten Gebäude gemessen werden.

Mit der Verleihung des Internationalen Hochhaus Preises begleitet das deutsche Architekturmuseum (DAM) die weltweit andauernde Entwicklung der architektonischen Paradedisziplin des 21. Jahrhunderts. Anhand der Projekte, die für den Internationalen Hochhaus Preis 2014 nominiert wurden, lässt sich der starke Trend hin zum Wohnhochhaus weiter bestätigen. Nachdem diese Wohnform in Asien schon lange der Standard für Besserverdienende ist, steigt die Nachfrage nach den USA nun auch in Europa. Ein Hauptaugenmerk liegt dabei vermehrt auf dem nachhaltigen, grünen Aspekt inmitten der Metropole. Weiterhin soll die zweijährliche Vergabe des Preises zur Dokumentation und Langzeitanalyse der zeitgenössischen Hochhausentwicklung dienen.

Deka Group. The real-estate business segment unites the group's real-estate competencies. The capital investment companies Deka Immobilien Investment GmbH and WestInvest Gesellschaft für Investmentfonds mbH are major investors in the European commercial property markets. The real-estate funds own more than 450 properties in 23 countries. As the investment management institution of the Sparkassen-Finanzgruppe, Deka Group feels it has a responsibility to engage in sustainable business principles, both ecologically and economically. In addition to the central investment maxim of profitability, sustainability is a significant criterion, and one that is also applied to the buildings nominated for the International Highrise Award.

Through the bestowal of the International Highrise Award the Deutsches Architekturmuseum (DAM) participates in the globally ongoing development of the prime architectural discipline of the twenty-first century. Looking at the projects that were nominated for the International Highrise Award in 2014, the strong trend for residential highrises is further corroborated. This way of living has long been the standard for high earners in Asia; now demand for it spilled over first to the United States, and is now on the way up in Europe. The sustainable, green aspect at the heart of the city has increasingly become a major focus of this development. The biennial award of this prize is also intended to serve the purpose of documenting and generating long-term analyses of contemporary highrise developments.

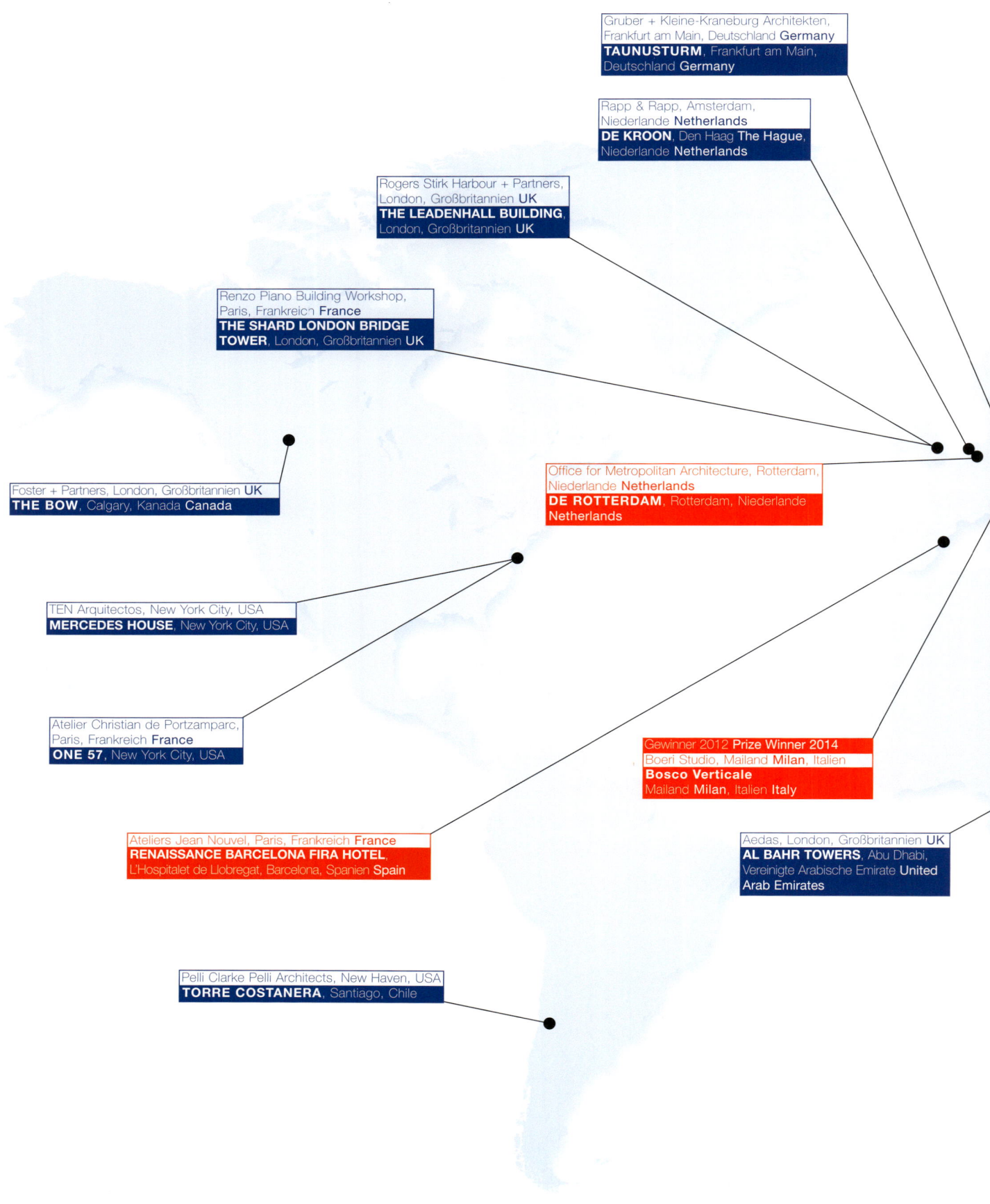

Gruber + Kleine-Kraneburg Architekten,
Frankfurt am Main, Deutschland Germany
TAUNUSTURM, Frankfurt am Main,
Deutschland Germany

Rapp & Rapp, Amsterdam,
Niederlande Netherlands
DE KROON, Den Haag The Hague,
Niederlande Netherlands

Rogers Stirk Harbour + Partners,
London, Großbritannien UK
THE LEADENHALL BUILDING,
London, Großbritannien UK

Renzo Piano Building Workshop,
Paris, Frankreich France
**THE SHARD LONDON BRIDGE
TOWER**, London, Großbritannien UK

Foster + Partners, London, Großbritannien UK
THE BOW, Calgary, Kanada Canada

Office for Metropolitan Architecture, Rotterdam,
Niederlande Netherlands
DE ROTTERDAM, Rotterdam, Niederlande
Netherlands

TEN Arquitectos, New York City, USA
MERCEDES HOUSE, New York City, USA

Atelier Christian de Portzamparc,
Paris, Frankreich France
ONE 57, New York City, USA

Gewinner 2012 **Prize Winner 2014**
Boeri Studio, Mailand **Milan**, Italien
Bosco Verticale
Mailand **Milan**, Italien **Italy**

Ateliers Jean Nouvel, Paris, Frankreich France
RENAISSANCE BARCELONA FIRA HOTEL,
L'Hospitalet de Llobregat, Barcelona, Spanien Spain

Aedas, London, Großbritannien UK
AL BAHR TOWERS, Abu Dhabi,
Vereinigte Arabische Emirate United
Arab Emirates

Pelli Clarke Pelli Architects, New Haven, USA
TORRE COSTANERA, Santiago, Chile

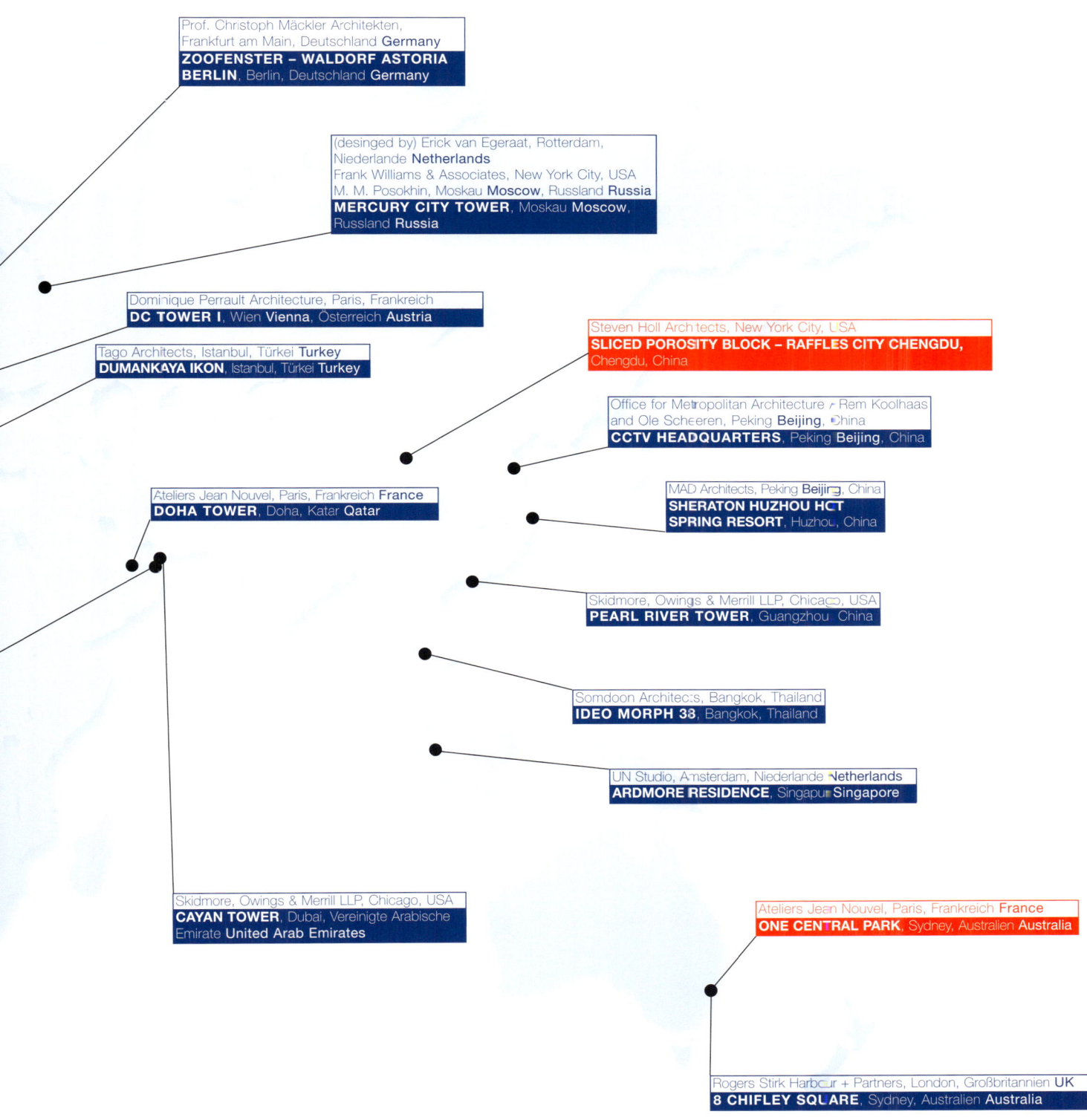

Prof. Christoph Mäckler Architekten,
Frankfurt am Main, Deutschland Germany
**ZOOFENSTER – WALDORF ASTORIA
BERLIN**, Berlin, Deutschland Germany

(desinged by) Erick van Egeraat, Rotterdam,
Niederlande **Netherlands**
Frank Williams & Associates, New York City, USA
M. M. Posokhin, Moskau **Moscow**, Russland **Russia**
MERCURY CITY TOWER, Moskau Moscow,
Russland **Russia**

Dominique Perrault Architecture, Paris, Frankreich
DC TOWER I, Wien Vienna, Österreich Austria

Tago Architects, Istanbul, Türkei **Turkey**
DUMANKAYA IKON, Istanbul, Türkei Turkey

Steven Holl Architects, New York City, USA
SLICED POROSITY BLOCK – RAFFLES CITY CHENGDU,
Chengdu, China

Office for Metropolitan Architecture – Rem Koolhaas
and Ole Scheeren, Peking **Beijing**, China
CCTV HEADQUARTERS, Peking Beijing, China

Ateliers Jean Nouvel, Paris, Frankreich **France**
DOHA TOWER, Doha, Katar Qatar

MAD Architects, Peking **Beijing**, China
**SHERATON HUZHOU HOT
SPRING RESORT**, Huzhou, China

Skidmore, Owings & Merrill LLP, Chicago, USA
PEARL RIVER TOWER, Guangzhou, China

Somdoon Architects, Bangkok, Thailand
IDEO MORPH 38, Bangkok, Thailand

UN Studio, Amsterdam, Niederlande **Netherlands**
ARDMORE RESIDENCE, Singapur Singapore

Skidmore, Owings & Merrill LLP, Chicago, USA
CAYAN TOWER, Dubai, Vereinigte Arabische
Emirate **United Arab Emirates**

Ateliers Jean Nouvel, Paris, Frankreich **France**
ONE CENTRAL PARK, Sydney, Australien Australia

Rogers Stirk Harbour + Partners, London, Großbritannien **UK**
8 CHIFLEY SQUARE, Sydney, Australien Australia

Finalist 2014

Steven Holl Architects
SLICED POROSITY BLOCK – RAFFLES CITY CHENGDU
Chengdu, China

Architekten **Architects** Steven Holl Architects, New York
Leitende Entwurfsarchitekten **Chief design architects** Steven Holl, Li Hu, Roberto Bannura (associate in charge)
Projektarchitekt Peking **Project architect Beijing** Lan Wu
Projektarchitekten New York **Project architects New York** Haiko Cornelissen, Peter Englaender, JongSeo Lee
Projektdesign **Project design** Christiane Deptolla, Inge Goudsmit, Jackie Luk, Maki Matsubayashi, Sarah Nichols, Manta Weihermann, Martin Zimmerli
Projektteam **Architectural team** Justin Allen, Jason Anderson, Francesco Bartolozzi, Guanlan Cao, Yimei Chan, Sofie Holm Christensen, Esin Erez, Ayat Fadaifard, Mingcheng Fu, Forrest Fulton, Runar Halldorsson, M. Emran Hossain, Joseph Kan, Suping Li, Tz-Li Lin, Yan Liu, Daijiro Nakayama, Pietro Peyron, Roberto Requejo, Elena Rojas-Danielsen, Michael Rusch, Ida Sze, Filipe Taboada, Ebbie Wisecarver, Human Tieliu Wu, Jin-Ling Yu
Lokale Architekten **Architects of record** China Academy of Building Research
Projektteam lokale Architekten **Team architects of record** Xue Ming, Wang Zhenming, Lu Yan
Bauherr **Client** CapitaLand
Tragwerksplanung **Structural engineers** China Academy of Building Research, Liu Junjin, Zhu Huosheng (Senior engineer)

Nachhaltigkeitskonzept **Sustainability concept** Transsolar
Lichtplanung **Lighting consultant** L'Observatoire International

Höhe **Height** 123 m
Geschosse **Floors** 35
Grundstücksfläche **Site area** 32 571 m²
Bebaute Fläche **Footprint** 17 883m²
Nettogeschossfläche **Net floor area** 310 000 m²
Konstruktion **Structure** Betonaußenskelett **Concrete exterior skeleton**
Fertigstellung **Completion** November 2013
Nutzung **Use** Büros, Wohnen, Einzelhandel, Cafés **Offices, residential, shops and cafés**
Ökologische Aspekte / Nachhaltigkeit **Ecological criteria / sustainability** Die Außenfassade dient als Wärmespeicher / Kältepuffer; Wasserflächen mit wiederaufbereitetem Regenwasser; natürliche Belichtung der unterirdischen Etagen; Heizung und Kühlung mittels 468 geothermal walls; energieeffiziente Haustechnik; Verwendung regionaler Baumaterialien. Die unregelmäßige Bauform reduziert die Verschattung der Umgebung. Nominiert für die LEED Gold Zertifizierung. **The exterior façade acts as a heat store / buffer from the cold; areas of water with treated rainwater; natural lighting in the underground floors; heating and cooling using 468 geothermal walls; energy-efficient domestic technology; use of regional construction materials. The irregular shape of the building reduces the amount of shade thrown on the surrounding area. Nominated for LEED Gold certification.**

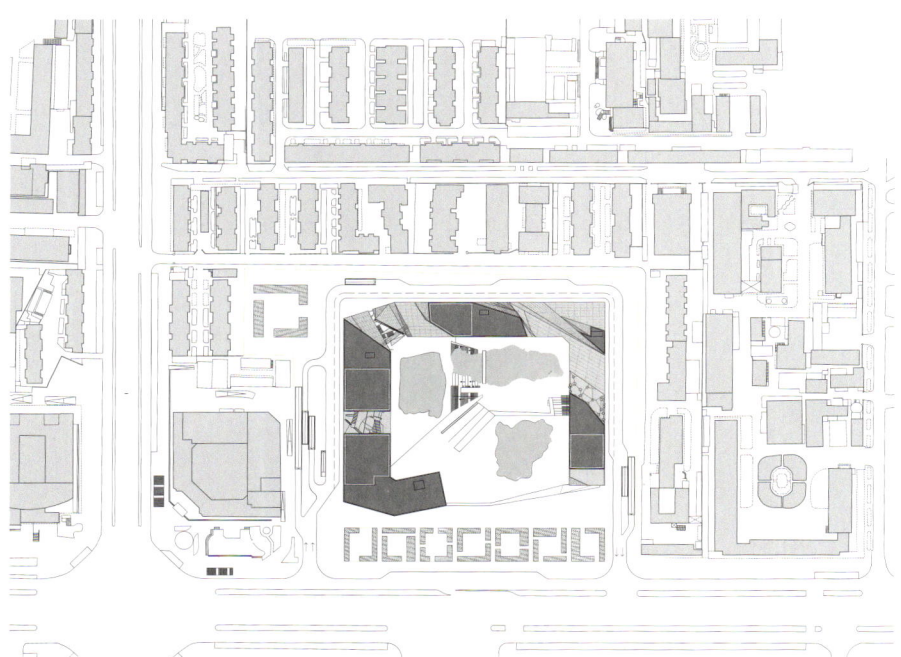

Lageplan **Site plan**

Der Hochhauskomplex überragt die angrenzende Bebauung, ist aber zugleich durch mehrere öffentliche Zugänge mit ihr verbunden.
The high-rise complex towers above the adjacent buildings but is connected to them through numerous public entrances.

Über teilweise begrünte Rampen und Treppen sind die verschieden öffentlichen Ebenen des Komplexes untereinander als auch mit der Umgebung verbunden.
Partially landscaped ramps and terraces connect the various public levels of the complex are connected to one and another and to their surroundings.

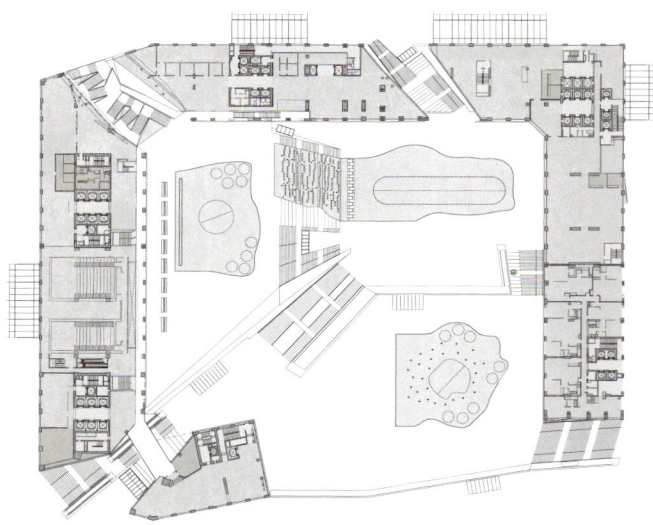

Grundriss 11. Obergeschoss mit innen liegendem Platz
Ground plan of the 11th floor with interior courtyard

Das Zentrum des Büro- und Wohnkomplexes Raffles City bildet ein großer Platz, um den fünf Hochhäuser gruppiert sind. Deren plastische Kubatur leitet sich aus dem Tageslichteinfall ab und resultiert in unregelmäßigen Fassadenformen mit spitzen und stumpfen Winkeln, Abschrägungen und mehrgeschossigen Auskragungen. Eine gleichmäßige Pfosten-Riegel-Konstruktion aus weißem Beton bildet die Außenhaut. Die Gitterstruktur wird von schräg liegenden Betonträgern durchschnitten, die an den Aussparungen oder Auskragungen statisch erforderlich werden und gleichzeitig zur Erdbebensicherheit beitragen. Mit der Verlagerung der Tragstruktur in die Außenhaut können im Inneren der Gebäude weitgehend stützenfreie Grundrisse erzielt werden. Geothermische Vorkehrungen, Sonnenschutzverglasung und eine energieeffiziente Ausstattung tragen zu Einsparungen und insbesondere zur Umweltverträglichkeit bei. Dabei wurden vorwiegend regionale Baumaterialien verwendet.

The heart of the Raffles City office and residential complex is a large open space around which five highrises are located. The plasticity of the blocks derives from the incidence of natural light, producing irregular façade shapes with acute and obtuse angles, slants and projections extending over several floors. A regular post-and-beam construction of white concrete forms the outer skin of the buildings. The grid structure is transected by diagonal concrete supports that perform a necessary load-bearing function at the recesses and projections, while at the same time contributing to the building's ability to withstand earthquakes. Moving the supporting structure to the exterior skin means that the interior can make do largely without supports. Geothermal provision, solar protection glazing and an energy-efficient interior all contribute to savings and to environmental sustainability. Beside that overwhelming majority of the building materials were regional.

Ostansicht **East elevation**

T4-Apartment
T-4 Apartment

T3-Hotel
T-3 Hotel

T2-Büro
T-2 Office

Entlang der das Grundstück begrenzenden Ren-Min-Nan-Straße ist die Bebauung niedriger angelegt und schafft somit einen Übergang zur kleinteiligen Wohnbebauung der Umgebung. Im Erdgeschoss gibt es kleine Läden, die sich sowohl zur Straße als auch zu einer innen liegenden Einkaufspassage und schließlich zum Platz hin öffnen. Dieser wird besonders in den Abendstunden mit Lichtspielen an den Fassaden zu einem spektakulären Erlebnisraum für das umliegende Quartier. Bei der Gestaltung ließen sich die Planer von dem aus Chengdu stammenden Dichter Du Fu (713–770) anregen. „Drei Täler" aus einem seiner Gedichte nehmen architektonisch die Form von drei Wasserflächen auf unterschiedlichen Bodenniveaus an. Bei Dunkelheit spiegeln sie die Lichteffekte an den Fassaden wider, am Tage dienen sie als Oberlichter für eine darunter liegende Einkaufspassage. Eine weitere Passage führt auf der 7. Etage durch die einzelnen Gebäude.

Insgesamt stellt die Konzeption dieser multifunktionalen Nachbarschaftssiedlung eine plastische Variante des 2008 von Steven Holl in Peking realisierten Linked Hybrid Wohnkomplexes dar.

Begründung der Jury
Bei dem Gebäudekomplex in Chengdu von Steven Holl Architects war die Jury besonders von der Intelligenz beeindruckt, mit der die Planer eine massive städtische Form nutzten, um einen geschützten öffentlichen Raum zu gestalten – und das mitten in einer sehr lebendigen, chaotischen Metropole. Dabei sind die Gebäude keine Festung, abgeschnitten von der Stadt: es gibt fünf Zugänge zum städtischen Umfeld damit auch Passanten von der Attraktivität dieses öffentlichen Raums profitieren können. Das Projekt ist ein höchst beeindruckender Prototyp für dicht bevölkerten Wohngebiete des modernen China.

The buildings are not so high along the Ren-Min-Nan Road, which borders the plot, thereby forming a transition to the smaller residential buildings of the surrounding area. There are small shops on the ground floor that open up both to the street and to an indoor shopping arcade and eventually to the interior quadrangle. During the evening hours, the latter becomes a spectacular event space for the surrounding neighbourhood when lights are projected on to the façades. The planners' designs were inspired by the poet Du Fu (713–770), himself from Chengdu. Architecturally, 'Three Valleys' from one of his poems take on the form of three surfaces of water at different levels. When it is dark, they reflect the light effects on the façades, during the day they serve as overhead lighting for the shopping arcade below. A further arcade runs through the individual buildings on the seventh floor.

Overall, the conception of this multi-functional neighbour-hood development is a more sculptural variant of the Linked Hybrid residential complex in Beijing, designed by Steven Holl in 2008.

Jury statement
What the jury appreciates about the scheme in Chengdu by Steven Holl Architects is the intelligence with which the designers have used a massively urban form to create a protected public space in the middle of a very busy, chaotic metropolis. At the same time it is not cut from the city, it is not a fortress, there are five links to the urban fabric that ensure that also passersby can benefit from the beauty of this public space. The project is an amazing prototype for the high-density developments of the current China right now.

Über die Wasserflächen zwischen den einzelnen Gebäuden werden die darunter liegenden Geschosse belichtet.
Expanses of water between the individual buildings illuminate the surrounding storeys.

Die fünf Hochhaustürme schützen einen Hort der Ruhe vor dem lauten und hektischen Verkehr der Umgebung.
The five high-rises tower above the small-scale construction of their surroundings and shelter a calm refuge from noise and hectic movement.

Finalist 2014

Ateliers Jean Nouvel
ONE CENTRAL PARK
Sydney, Australien **Australia**

Architekten **Architects** Ateliers Jean Nouvel, Paris
Leitender Entwurfsarchitekt **Chief design architect** Jean
Nouvel
Leitende Architekten **Project directors** Bertram Beissel,
Emmanuel Blamont, Terry Brabazon, Paul Van
Ratingen, Brian Wait
Projektleiter **Project leaders** Hakan Aldogan, Elisabeth
Kather, Didier Lobjois (Assistent **Assistant**)
Projektteam **Architectural team** Roula Akiki, Arnaud
Brichet, Arnaud Coutine, Sara Hearne, Narjis Lemrini,
Clément Meurisse, Justine Puyaubreau, Emmanuelle
Stalla-Bourdillon, Nobuo Yoshida, Qiang Zou
Lokale Architekten **Architects of record** PTW Architects
(Peddle Thorp & Walker), Sydney
Bauherr **Client** Frasers Property Australia; Sekisui
House Australia
Landschaftsarchitekten **Landscape architects** Ewen Le
Ruic, Irene Djao-Rakitine, Celine Aubernais
Bepflanzung Terrassen **Planting, terraces** Aspect
Oculus
Pflanzenwände **Green walls** Patrick Blanc
Heliostat-Design Kennovations
LED Design Yann Kersalé
Tragwerksplanung **Structural engineers** Robert Bird
Group
Haustechnik **MEP** Arup
Nachhaltigkeitskonzept **Sustainability concept**
Transsolar

Höhe **Height** 116 m und **and** 64,5 m
Geschosse **Floors** 34 und **and** 17
Grundstücksfläche **Site area** 25 5500 m²
Bebaute Fläche **Footprint** 7550 m²
Bruttogeschossfläche **Gross floor area** 67 626 m²
Konstruktion **Structure** Stahl und Beton **Steel and
concrete**
Fertigstellung **Completion** September 2012
Nutzung **Use** Wohnen und Einzelhandel **Residential
and retail**
Ökologische Aspekte / Nachhaltigkeit **Ecological
criteria / sustainability** Nachhaltige Stadtentwicklung
durch Verdichtung und Begrünung des Stadtraums; die
Begrünung der Fassaden führt zu Absorbierung von
Staubpartikeln und CO₂, Produktion von Sauerstoff,
Verbesserung des Mikroklimas; natürliche Verschattung
der Balkone und Wohnungen; Reduzierung des
Energieverbrauchs um 25 Prozent; Bewässerung mit
Grau- und Schwarzwasser; integriertes TriGen-
Kraftwerk zur Speicherung von Solarenergie; Heliostat-
System zur Belichtung verschatteter Bereiche.
Sustainable urban development through densification
and more plants in the urban space; green façades to
absorb dust particles and carbon dioxide, to produce
oxygen and to improve the microclimate; natural shade
for the balconies and flats; 25% energy reduction;
irrigation with greywater and blackwater; integrated
TriGen power station to store solar energy; heliostat
system to light up shady areas.

Das begrünte Wohnhochhaus steht auf dem Gelände
der ehemaligen Carlton and United-Brauerei, einem
städtischen Revitalisierungsgebiet nahe dem Hauptbahnhof von Sydney. Es kommt den im Bebauungsplan
der Stadt vorgesehenen Verdichtungen an Verkehrsknotenpunkten entgegen, denn eine höhere und
nachhaltige Wohnbebauung soll zukünftig den
Landverbrauch in der Umgebung Sydneys reduzieren
und das Leben in der Stadt attraktiver machen.

This residential highrise with its green walls stands on
the plot of the former Carlton and United Brewery, an
urban regeneration area near Sydney's central station.
It plays to the city's planning ideas of densification
near major transport hubs, because the intention is for
higher and sustainable residential construction to
reduce land use around Sydney and make life in the
city more attractive.

Die Fassade wird durch die umlaufende Begrünung in Form von kleinen Balkonen horizontal gegliedert. Aufgebrochen wird diese Gliederung durch vertikale Pflanzenwände von Patrick Blanc. Bereits 2005 integrierte Jean Nouvel eine große Pflanzenwand des Grünkünstlers am Musée du Quai Branly in Paris.

The façade is subdivided horizontally by all-around greening in the form of small balconies. This structure is broken up by vertical green walls designed by Patrick Blanc. In 2005, Jean Nouvel also integrated one of the botanical artist's large vertical gardens into the Musée du Quai Branly in Paris.

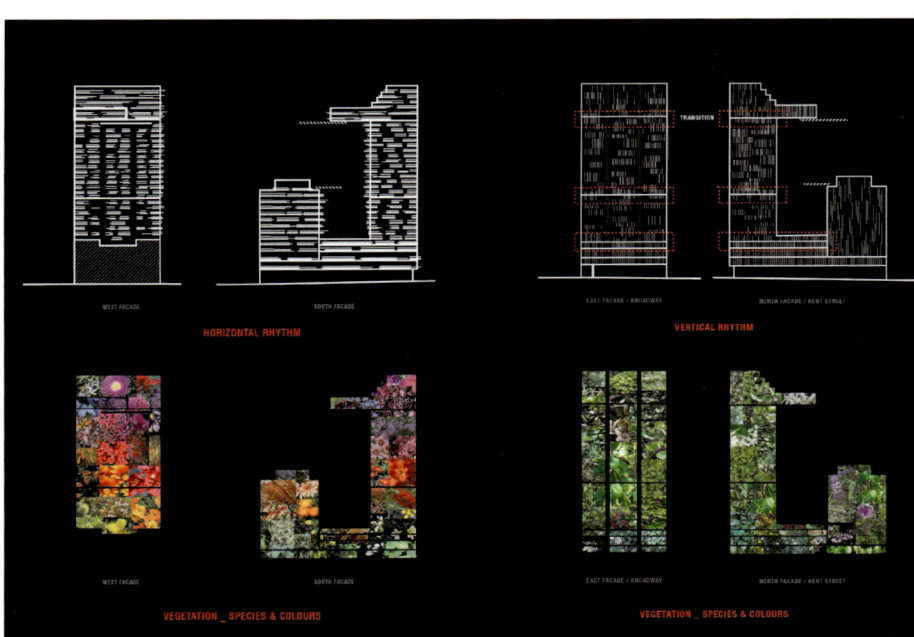

Schnitt mit Tageslichtführung
Cutaway view showing daylight management

Mit dem Einsetzen der Dunkelheit wird der Komplex durch eine in den Heliostat integrierte Lichtinstallation des französischen Künstlers Yann Kersalé farbig illuminiert.
Integrated into the heliostat, a colourful light installation by French artist Yann Kersalé illuminates the complex after dark.

Das aus zwei Türmen bestehende Gebäude basiert auf einem trapezförmigen Grundriss. Die beiden 65 und 116 Meter hohen Baukörper stehen auf einem gemeinsamen Sockelbau und werden durch einen Zwischenraum getrennt. Dieser liegt weitgehend im Schatten und kann mit Hilfe einer ausgefeilten Tageslichttechnik natürlich belichtet werden. Auf der Dachfläche des niedrigen Baublocks befinden sich 42 Sonnenreflektorschirme (*heliostats*), die Sonnenlicht auf einen mit Reflektoren bestückten Ausleger an der 29. Etage des höheren Gebäudeteils werfen. Dieser reflektiert das Licht nach unten in den Zwischenraum und gleichzeitig auf einen nördlich des Gebäudes gelegenen Park, der ansonsten durch das Hochhaus weitgehend verschattet würde.

The building, which consists of two towers, is based on a trapezoid ground plan. The two structures, 65m and 116 m high, stand on a shared foundation and are separated from each other by an interspace. This space is largely in shadow and can be illuminated with natural light using ingenious daylight technology. There are 42 heliostats (sunlight reflectors) on the roof of the lower of the two towers; they reflect sunlight on to an extension on the 29th floor of the higher tower, which is also fitted with reflectors. This extension reflects the light downwards into the interspace as well as on to a park to the north of the building that would otherwise be largely in shadow because of the highrise.

One Central Park bildet das Herz eines neuen Bezirks, der über 6500 m² Park und öffentlichen Raum verfügt.
One Central Park forms the heart of the new district, which include over 6500 square metres of parks and public space.

Das besondere Merkmal des Gebäudes ist seine umlaufende Begrünung. Entlang der Etagen sind bepflanzte Balkone angelegt und an den Fassadenflächen gibt es Pflanzenwände, die der natürlichen Verschattung und Kühlung der dahinter liegenden Wohnungen dienen. Besonders während der heißen Sommermonate können dadurch Energieeinsparungen von bis zu 30% erreicht werden. Die Pflanzen verarbeiten Kohlendioxid und produzieren Sauerstoff, was sich positiv auf das Klima der Umgebung auswirkt. Zudem werden sie mit Grau- und sogar mit Schwarzwasser versorgt. Angesichts der Wasserknappheit in Sydney stellt dies einen großen Vorteil dar.

In seiner Konzeption orientiert sich das Projekt an den hohen Standards des Australian Green Star für umweltverträglichen und energieeffizienten Wohnungsbau.

Begründung der Jury
Bei One Central Park führt der geniale Einsatz von moderner Umwelttechnik zu einer dicht bewohnbaren Siedlung auf einer eng begrenzten Fläche. Darüber hinaus hat das Team von Jean Nouvel das Gebäude durchgehend begrünt. Ganz gleich wo man sich im Gebäude befindet, spürt man das Grün der Außenwelt – und das ist bei Hochhäusern keine Selbstverständlichkeit. Die erfolgreiche Entwicklung dieses Standorts in Sydney ist sehr spannend und durchaus ein Modell für Gebäude dieser Art im 21. Jahrhundert.

The building's special feature is its comprehensive use of plants. There are planted balconies, while the green walls of the façades provide natural shading and cooling for the flats behind them. During the hot summer months, this can bring about energy savings of up to 30% . The plants process carbon dioxide and produce oxygen, which has a positive impact on the climate of the surrounding area. In addition they are supplied with greywater and even blackwater. Bearing in mind that Sydney is not abundantly supplied with water, this is a great advantage.

The project's design took as a criterion the high standard of the Australian Green Star for environmental and energy-efficient residential construction.

Jury statement
At One Central Park an ingenious use of environmental engineering produces a very high density project on a restricted site. On top of that Ateliers Jean Nouvel have greened the building throughout. So wherever you are in the building you would still be reading the greenery of the outside world; not common necessary in tower buildings. The project is very exciting in its very successful development for the site in Sydney and definitely a model for a building of this type in the 21st century.

Die Begrünung der Fassaden, Balkone und Terrassen dient nicht nur der Verschattung, sondern bietet Aufenthaltsqualität für die Bewohner.
Greening on the façades, balconies and terraces provides both shade and quality of life.

Finalist 2014

Ateliers Jean Nouvel

RENAISSANCE BARCELONA FIRA HOTEL

L'Hospitalet de Llobregat, Barcelona, Spanien **Spain**

Architekten **Architects** Ateliers Jean Nouvel, Paris
Leitender Entwurfsarchitekt **Chief design architect** Jean Nouvel
Leitende Projektarchitekten **Chief project architects** Emmanuel Blamont, José Miguel Pomares, Damien Renchon
Projektarchitekten **Project architects** Markus Frank, Eric Nespoulos, Joan Pau, Yasmina Perez, Gonzalo Ruiz, Victor Sanchez, Julia Tupper, Fina Urpi
Ausführende Architekten **Contracting architects** Gregoire Giot, Pau Gomez, Jeremy Lebarillec, Cristina Perales, Adriana Ribas, Cristina Sanchez, Jordi Sinfreu, Yvonne Weber, EMA
Lokale Architekten **Architects of record** Ribas & Ribas Arquitectos
Innenarchitektur **Interior design** Sabrina Letourneur, Jean Nouvel Design
Bauherr **Client** Hoteles Catalonia
Tragwerksplanung **Structural engineers** Manuel Arguijo y asociados, S.L.
Haustechnik **MEP** Ramón Roca

Höhe **Height** 105 m
Geschosse **Floors** 27
Grundstücksfläche **Site area** 4000 m²
Bebaute Fläche **Footprint** 975 m²
Nettogeschossfläche **Net floor area** 22 000 m²
Konstruktion **Structure** Beton, Stahl, Glas **Concrete, steel, glass**
Fertigstellung **Completion** September 2012
Nutzung **Use** Hotel
Ökologische Aspekte / Nachhaltigkeit **Ecological criteria / sustainability** Begrünung und Durchlüftung des offenen Zwischenraums; dadurch natürliche Kühlung der Etagen; an den Außenfassaden effektvolle Verschattung der Innenräume; Photovoltaik; Dachbegrünung; Verwendung heimischer Pflanzen und Baumaterialien; Erdbebensicherheit durch „tuned mass dumper". Nominiert für die Auszeichnung LEED Gold oder Platin. **Planting and ventilation of the open intermediate space; therefore natural cooling of the floors; effective shading of the rooms on the exterior façades; solar panels; green roof; use of native plants and building materials; earthquake security through tuned mass dumper. Nominated for the LEED award in gold or platinum.**

Das aus zwei parallel angeordneten Hochhausscheiben bestehende Hotel befindet sich in L'Hospitalet de Llobregat, einem Stadtteil im Süden Barcelonas. Umgeben von einem Palmenwäldchen grenzt es an den neu geschaffenen Plaza Europa.

Die Außenfassaden des 105 Meter hohen Gebäudes sind an drei Seten weiß verkleidet, an der Schmalseite zum Platz hin, wo sich auch der Eingang befindet, matt schwarz. Die Fassaden werden nicht durch Fensterreihen, sondern durch ein Muster aus unregelmäßig gestalteten Öffrungen, die an Palmenblätter erinnern, strukturiert. Die Umrisse dieser Öffnungen setzen sich als „esgrafiados" auf den angrenzenden Betonflächen fort. In den Zimmern entstehen Schattenwürfe, die sich je nach Lichteinfall verändern und an „ombres chinoises" südostasiatischer Schattenspiele denken lassen. Die insgesamt 358 Gästezimmer unterscheiden sich aufgrund dieser Lichteffekte voneinander, sind aber auch in Größe und Ausstattung unterschiedlich konzipiert.

The hotel, consisting of two parallel highrise slabs, is located in L'Hospitalet de Llobregat, a district in the south of Barcelona. Surrounded by a palm grove, it borders the newly built Plaza Europa.

The exterior façades of the 105-metre-tall building are white on three sides, while the narrow side that faces the square, which is also the side where the entrance is located, is matt black. The façades are not structured by rows of windows but instead by a pattern of irregular openings that resemble palm leaves. The outlines of these openings continue as 'esgrafiados' on the adjoining concrete surfaces. The shadows created in the rooms change depending on the direction of the incident light; they are reminiscent of the 'ombres chinoises' of Chinese shadow puppetry. The 358 rooms differ from each other because of these light effects, but they also vary in size and interior appointments.

Während sich die Fassade am Atrium öffnet, verschattet die Struktur aus Palmenblättern die Hotelzimmer und schützt sie vor Sonneneinstrahlung. Zugleich verweist das Motiv auf das Grün im Inneren des Hotels.
While the façade opens onto the atrium, the palm-leaf structure provides shade to the hotel rooms and protects them from direct sunlight. At the same time, the motif makes reference to the green in the hotel's interior.

Vorbei an vertikalen Gärten führen frei tragende Stahltreppen
und -brücken durch das Atrium zu den Hotelzimmern. Auf dem
Weg kann man den luftigen Blick über Barcelona genießen.
Passing by vertical gardens, self-supporting steel staircases
and bridges lead guests through the atrium to the hotel
rooms. Along the way, one can enjoy the lofty view over
Barcelona.

Ein die Hochhausscheiben trennender Abstandsraum ist offen und luftdurchlässig. Die Balustraden entlang der Stockwerke sind bepflanzt und bilden hängende Gärten. Brücken und offene Treppen im Zwischenraum dienen als Querverbindungen und ermöglichen Ausblicke auf die umgebende Stadtlandschaft. Der Austritt aus dem Hotelzimmer führt nicht auf einen geschlossenen Korridor, sondern in einen luftigen Schattenraum, in dem die Umgänge und Treppen eine an Piranesi erinnernde verwirrende Struktur entstehen lassen. Der Zwischenraum ist schattig und kühl und die in einem Hochhaus generell üblichen Windlasten sind im sommerlich heißen Klima Nordspaniens durchaus willkommen.

An atrium separating the two highrise slabs is open and air-permeable. The balustrades along the floors are full of plants and have become hanging gardens. Walkways and open staircases in the atrium are used as connectors, while also being good vantage points for views of the surrounding cityscape. When leaving their hotel room, guests do not find themselves in a closed corridor; instead they enter an airy, shady space in which the galleries and stairs create a confusing structure reminiscent of Piranesi. The atrium is shady and cool and the wind forces that are typical of highrises are quite welcome in the hot summer climate of northern Spain.

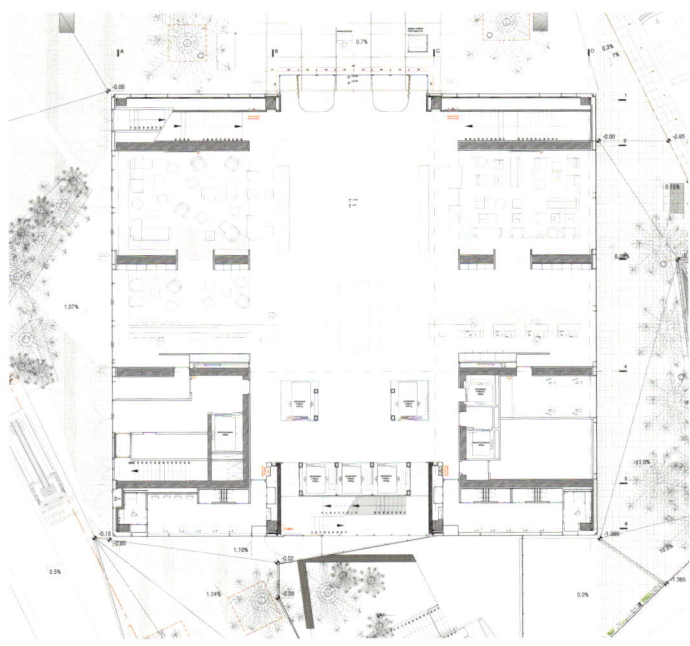

Grundriss Erdgeschoss
Ground floor plan

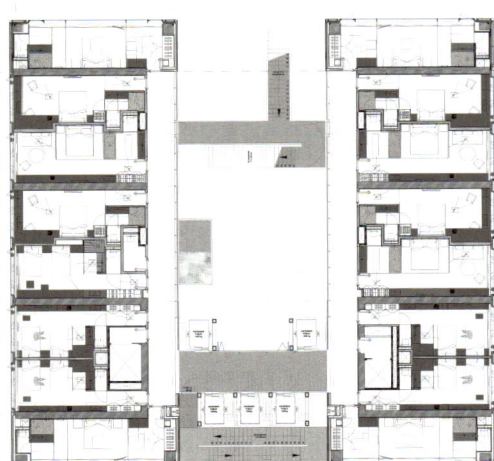

Grundriss Regelgeschoss
Typical floor plan

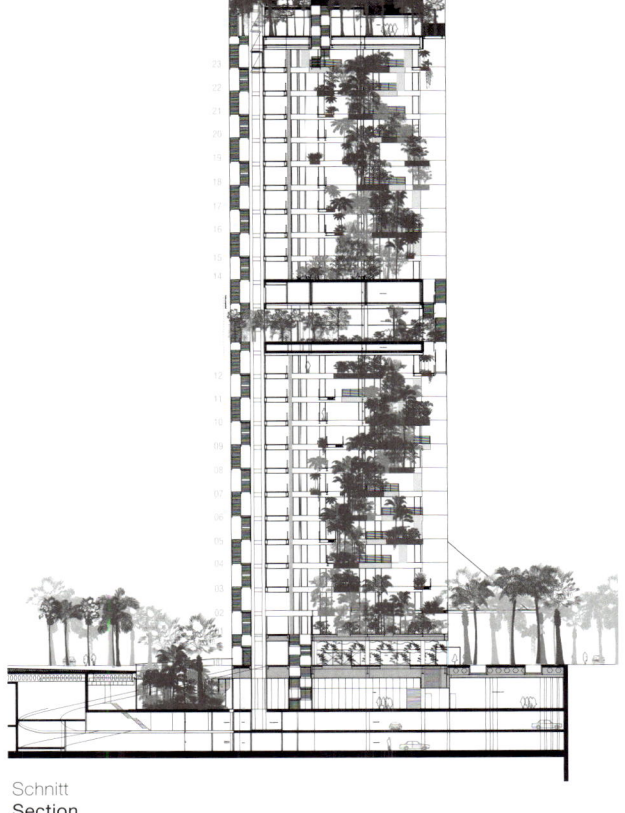

Schnitt
Section

Das 14. Stockwerk ist einem Restaurant vorbehalten. Hier, wie auch im Dachgeschoss, wurden die Bodenplatten über den Zwischenraum hinweggeführt und funktionieren als Verklammerung der beiden Hochhausscheiben. Auf dem Dachgeschoss finden sich die Palmen wieder, die hier ein Schwimmbad und verschiedene Fitnessbereiche beschatten.

Begründung der Jury
Das Gebäude repräsentiert eine neue Typologie des Hotelbaus. Dieser Entwurf ermöglicht es dem Gast, einfach aus seinem Hotelzimmer direkt in einen bepflanzten Gang unter freiem Himmel zu gehen, hinein in die warme Atmosphäre Barcelonas – in einen Gang ohne hermetische Abriegelung, künstliches Licht oder Klimaanlage. Auf diese Art erzeugt das Gebäude einen Dialog zwischen Innen- und Außenwelt. Dank des breiten Raums zwischen den beiden Hochhausscheiben spürt der Besucher die Höhe des Gebäudes.

The 14th storey is reserved for a restaurant. Here, as well as on the top floor, the floors project over the atrium, acting as a bracket for the two highrise slabs. The top floor features palm trees that provide shade for a pool and various fitness areas.

Jury statement
The building is a new typology of a hotel. This particular design allows the visitor just to walk around his hotel room straight into the open-air garden corridor in the warmth of the Barcelona environment, a corridor that is not hermetically sealed, not artificially lit, not air-conditioned. So the building creates a dialogue between inside and outside and the visitor understands the height of the building due to its large space between the two sides.

Auf dem Dach des Gebäudes befindet sich ein Schwimmbad
mit einem beeindruckenden Ausblick für die Hotelgäste.
**The swimming pool on the building's roof offers hotel
guests an impressive view.**

Finalist 2014

Office for Metropolitan Architecture
DE ROTTERDAM
Rotterdam, Niederlande **Netherlands**

Architekten **Architects** Office for Metropolitan
Architecture, Rotterdam
Leitende Entwurfsarchitekten **Chief design architects**
Rem Koolhaas, Reinier de Graaf, Ellen van Loon
Projektleiter **Project manager** Kees van Casteren
Bauherr **Client** De Rotterdam CV
Tragwerksplanung **Structural engineers** Corsmit
Haustechnik **MEP** Techniplan (Büros **Offices**, Hotel),
Valstar Simonis, Rijswijk (Wohnungen, Sockel
Apartments, Base)
Fassadenplanung **Façade planning** Permasteelisa,
Middelburg (Büros **Offices**, Hotel, Sockel **Base**); TGM,
Asten (Wohnungen **Apartments**)

Höhe **Height** 151 m
Geschosse **Floors** 45
Grundstücksfläche **Site area** 3875 m²
Bebaute Fläche **Footprint** 3875 m²

Bruttogeschossfläche **Gross floor area** 162 807 m²
Nettogeschossfläche **Net floor area** 138 390 m²
Konstruktion **Structure** Beton **Concrete**
Fertigstellung **Completion** November 2013
Nutzung **Use** Büros, Wohnen, Hotel, Restaurants
Offices, residential, hotel, restaurants
Ökologische Aspekte / Nachhaltigkeit **Ecological
criteria / sustainability** Vertikale Stadt; kurze Wege zu
unterschiedlichen urbanen Aktivitäten führen zu
Verringerung des Energieverbrauchs (Verkehr,
Transport); geschosshohe Verglasung zur optimalen
Tageslichtnutzung; Tageslichtreflektoren; LED-Beleuch-
tung in den öffentlichen Bereichen; Blockheizkraftwerk
plus Einspeisung von Bio-Kraftstoff; Nutzung von
Flusswasser zur Kühlung; flexibles umnutzungsfähiges
Raumprogramm. **Vertical city; short distances to
different urban activities lead to a reduction in energy
use (traffic, transport); floor-to-ceiling windows to
maximize the use of daylight; daylight reflectors;
LED lighting in the public areas; CHP unit plus feeding
of bio-fuel; use of river water for cooling; flexible
space allocation capable of conversion.**

Wie ein Massiv erhebt sich der aus drei Türmen
bestehende Hochhauskomplex auf dem Wilhelmina-
Pier im ehemaligen Hafen von Rotterdam. In seinem
Maßstab korrespondiert das Bauwerk nur mit dem
markanten Pfeiler der Erasmusbrücke, nicht aber mit
der kleinteiligen historischen Bebauung des
ehemaligen Hafengebiets. Davon ist allerdings nicht
mehr viel erhalten, denn der Hafen wurde im Zweiten
Weltkrieg stark zerstört und hat sich in den
vergangenen Jahren zu einem der erfolgreichsten
Hafenkonvertierungsprojekte Europas entwickelt.

The highrise complex, which consists of three towers,
rises up like a mountain range on the Wilhelmina Pier
in Rotterdam's former harbour. The building's scale
corresponds only to the striking pillar of the Erasmus
Bridge, but not to the smaller historic buildings of the
former harbour area. Not much is left of them,
however, because the harbour was largely destroyed
during the Second World War; in recent years it has
developed into one of Europe's most successful dock
conversion projects.

Während der Fahrt über die Erasmusbrücke vom Amsterdamer Büro UN Studio
türmt sich das Hochhausensemble beeindruckend vor den Passanten auf.
**During the drive across the Erasmus Bridge – designed by Amsterdam's
UN Studio – the high-rise ensemble towers imposingly in front of passers-by.**

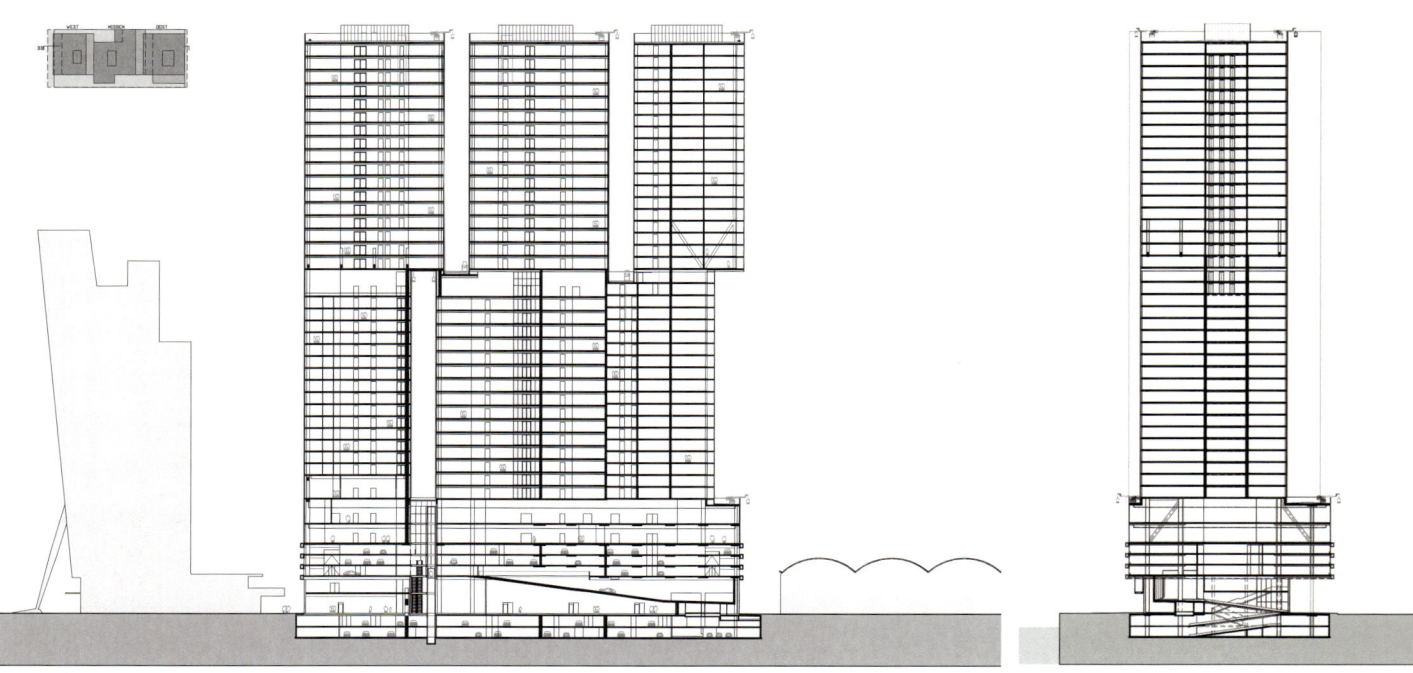

Längs- und Querschnitt
Longitudinal and transverse sections

Aus dem Hochhaus und von den Balkonen entlang der Schmalseite des Gebäudes haben die Bewohner einen unverbauten Blick über die Maas und das Zentrum von Rotterdam.
From the high-rise and along the narrow side of the building, residents have an unobstructed view across the Maas and the centre of Rotterdam.

Rem Koolhaas' Spezialität ist es, Superlative zu schaffen. Seine Bauten haben dennoch immer einen städtebaulichen Bezug. So orientiert sich auch De Rotterdam an der Idee einer „vertikalen Stadt", deren vielfältige Funktionen sichtbar übereinander gestapelt scheinen. Im Verlauf der langen Planungszeit mussten an der Konzeption seit 1997 allerdings immer mehr Abstriche gemacht werden. Die Büroräume, die inzwischen von der Stadtverwaltung Rotterdams bezogen wurden, sind auf Minimalstandards reduziert. Gleiches gilt für die 240 Wohnungen bis zum 44. Obergeschoss und für die 285 Zimmer eines im östlichen Turm angesiedelten Hotels.

It is Rem Koolhaas's speciality to create structures of a superlative nature. Nevertheless, his buildings always have a relationship to their urban context. Thus De Rotterdam is also geared to the idea of a 'vertical city', whose diverse functions are seen to be layered on top of each other. However, over the course of the long planning period, which started in 1997, the design had to be reduced more and more. The offices, which are now home to Rotterdam's city administration, have been reduced to minimal standards. The same is true of the 240 flats up to the 44th floor and for the 285 rooms in a hotel in the eastern tower.

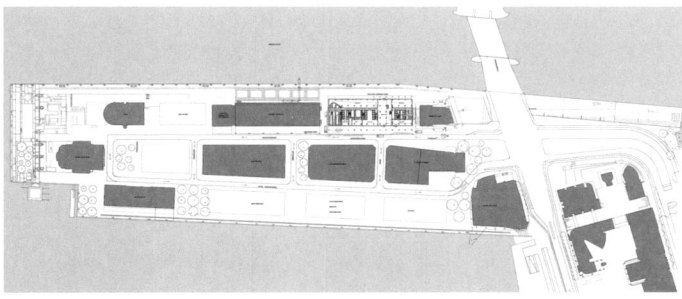

Lageplan
Site plan

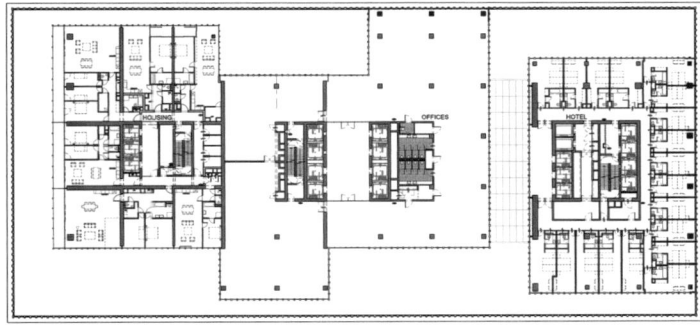

Grundriss Regelgeschoss unterer Teil
Typical floor plan lower part

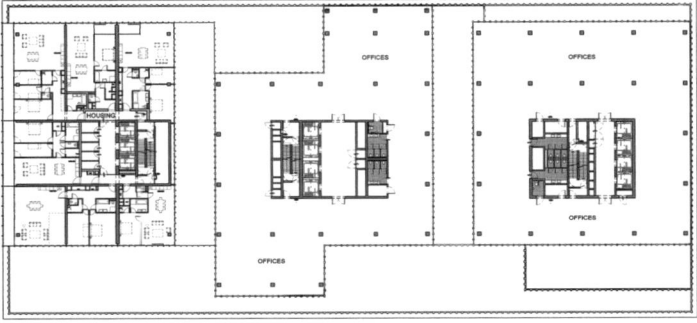

Grundriss Regelgeschoss oberer Teil
Typical floor plan upper part

Blick aus dem Foyer hinauf zwischen die Türme
View from the foyer between the towers

Im 30 Meter hohen Sockelbau ist auf sechs Etagen ein Parkhaus untergebracht. Ein weiträumiges Eingangsfoyer bietet im Erdgeschoss Zugang zu einem Kongresszentrum sowie zu Restaurants, Bars und Fitnessstudios. Doch auch hier wurde die Gestaltung auf funktional Notwendiges zurückgenommen. Geblieben sind einige spektakuläre Blickachsen nach oben und die Sicht aus der großzügig verglasten Fensterfront auf die vorbeifließende Maas.

Die aufgehenden Fassaden sind mit einer filigran wirkenden, je nach Betrachterstandpunkt changierenden, Pfosten-Riegel-Konstruktion aus Aluminium verkleidet. Sie verleiht dem Gesamtkomplex, dessen einzelne Baukörper durch schmale Zwischenräume voneinander getrennt sind, eine vereinheitlichende Hülle.

Begründung der Jury
De Rotterdam erweitert die Dimensionen der Stadt; gleichzeitig ist der Komplex eine Art Prädiktion der Bevölkerungsdichte der Zukunft und ein Modell für multifunktionele Stadtprojekte auf der ganzen Welt. Ein so hohes Niveau plastischer Eleganz wird aber an einem anderen Ort schwer zu realisieren sein.

The 30-metre-tall structure that forms the foot of all three towers houses a parking garage over six floors. An expansive entrance foyer on the ground floor provides access to a conference centre, as well as to restaurants, bars and gyms. But here too the design has been reduced to the functionally necessary. What remains are some spectacular lines of sight upwards and the view from the generously glazed façade on to the River Maas which flows by in front of it.

The rising façades are clad in an aluminium post-and-beam construction that has a filigree feel and seems to change depending on the location of the beholder. It gives the entire complex, whose individual structures are separated from each other by narrow interspaces, a unifying envelope.

Jury statement
De Rotterdam is opening the scale of the city on the one hand and is a prediction of future density as a model of mixed-use projects for many cities in the world. It will be hard to reach such a level of sculptural elegance as this project has executed again in another place.

Materialien wie Beton, Metall und Glas unterstreichen die strenge Formensprache auch im Inneren des Gebäudes.
Materials such as concrete, metal and glass reinforce the severe formal language in the building's interior as well.

Anhand einer Vielzahl von Arbeitsmodellen wurde die finale Form gefunden.
The final form was chosen based on a variety of working models.

Nominiertes Projekt 2014
Nominated Project 2014

Aedas UK
AL BAHR TOWERS
Abu Dhabi, Vereinigte Arabische Emirate **United Arab Emirates**

Architekten **Architects** Aedas, London, Großbritannien **UK**
Bauherr **Client** Abu Dhabi Investment Council

Höhe **Hight** 145 m
Geschosse **Floors** 25
Grundstücksfäche **Site area** 21 770 m²

Bebaute Fläche **Footprint** 11 915 m²
Nettogeschossfläche **Net floor area** 52 000 m²
Konstruktion **Structure** Stahlbetonkern mit Stahlaußenskelett **Reinforced concrete core and perimeter steel frame**
Fertigstellung **Completion** September 2013
Nutzung **Use** Büros **Offices**
Ökologische Aspekte / Nachhaltigkeit **Ecological criteria / sustainability** Bewegliches Verschattungssystem zur Vermeidung direkter Sonnenlichteinstrahlung; Energieeinsparungen durch natürliche Belichtung und reduzierte Klimatisierung. **Mobile shading system to avoid direct sunlight falling into the building; energy savings through natural lighting and reduced air-conditioning.**

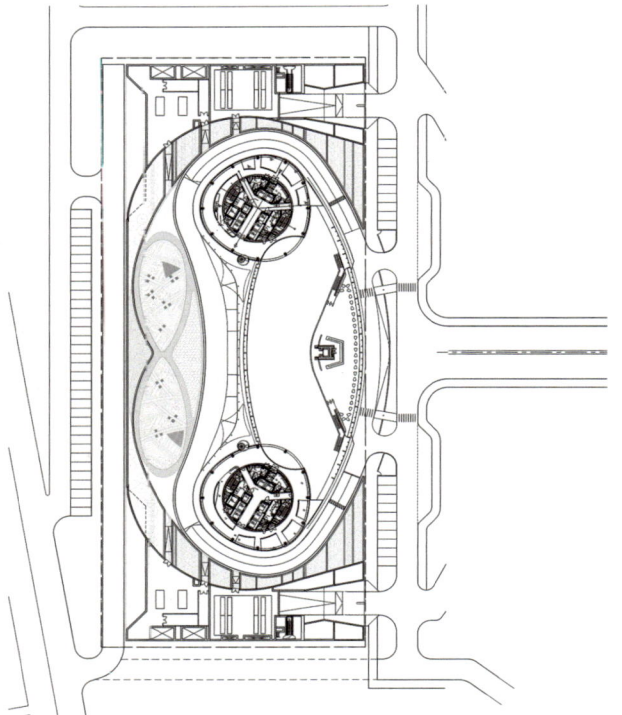

Lageplan **Site plan**

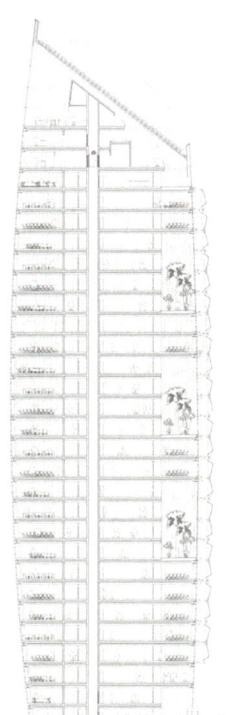

Schnitt **Section**

Die beiden Bürotürme am Stadtrand von Abu Dhabi zeichnen sich durch ihre innovativen Fassaden aus, die auf Forschungen zur „Bioinspiration" basieren. Einer einfachen Verglasung ist ein gitterartiges Verschattungssystem vorgelagert. Es hat tragende Funktion, passt sich automatisch dem jeweiligen Sonnenstand an und sorgt so für eine gleichmäßige diffuse Belichtung. In seinem Erscheinungsbild erinnert es an *mashrabiya*-Fenstergitter traditioneller arabischer Wohnbauten.

The two office towers on the outskirts of Abu Dhabi stand out thanks to their innovative façades based on 'bio inspiration' research. A simple glass façade is covered in a lattice-like shading system, which has a load-bearing function and automatically adapts to the amount of sunlight, creating a uniform, diffuse lighting environment. Its appearance is reminiscent of the *mashrabiya* window screens found in traditional Arabian homes.

Nominiertes Projekt 2014
Nominated Project 2014

(designed by) Erick van Egeraat
Frank Williams & Partners
MERCURY CITY TOWER
Moskau **Moscow**, Russland **Russia**

Architekten **Architects** Frank Williams & Partners, New
York (Gesamtentwurf **Total design**); (designed by) Erick
van Egeraat, Rotterdam (Entwurf Turmspitze **Design of
tower pinnacle**)
Projektarchitekt **Project architect** Erick van Egeraat
Lokale Architekten **Architects of record** Michail M.
Posokhin, Moskau **Moscow**
Bauherr **Client** Mercury Group

Höhe **Height** 339 m
Geschosse **Floors** 75
Grundstücksfläche **Site area** 4975 m²
Bebaute Fläche **Footprint** 3482 m²
Nettogeschossfläche **Net floor area** 173 960 m²

Konstruktion **Structure** Ortbeton **Cast-in-place concrete**
Fertigstellung **Completion** Juli **July** 2013
Nutzung **Use** Büros, Wohnen, Einzelhandel **Offices,
residential and retail**
Ökologische Aspekte / Nachhaltigkeit **Ecological
criteria / sustainability** Energieeffizient getönte
Glasfassade; hoher Tageslichtanteil in den Büros;
Reduzierung des Wasserverbrauchs durch Nutzung
von Brauchwasser.
Energy-efficient, tinted-glass façade; high percentage
of daylight in the offices; reduced water consumption
through use of industrial water.

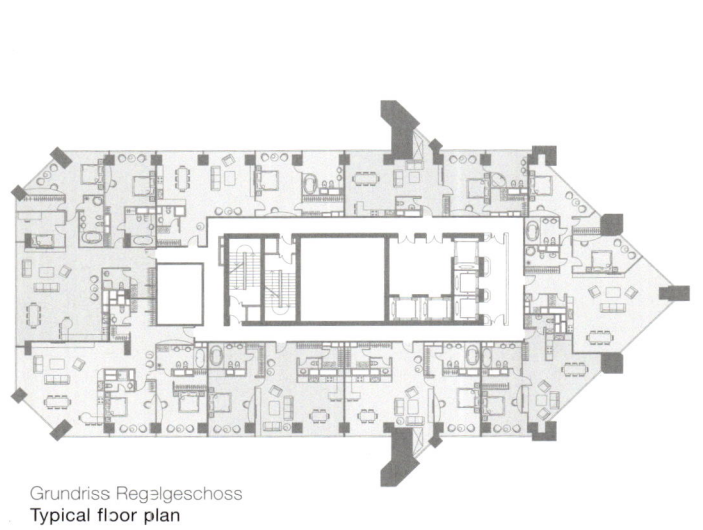

Grundriss Regelgeschoss
Typical floor plan

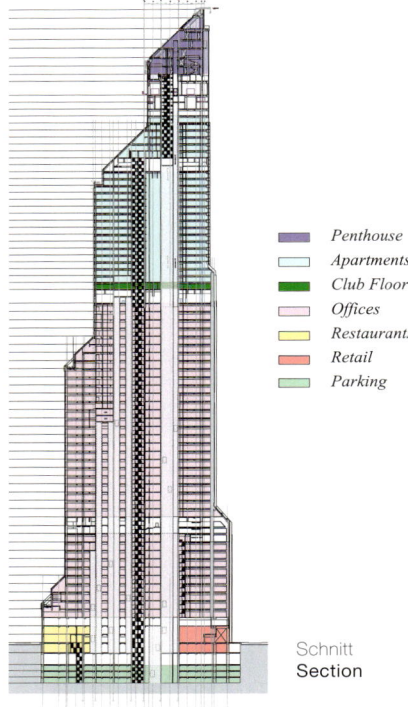

Penthouse
Apartments
Club Floor
Offices
Restaurants
Retail
Parking

Schnitt
Section

Das nach oben hin markant abgetreppte Hochhaus im
Geschäftsviertel von Moskau ist zurzeit das höchste
Gebäude in Europa und das erste umweltfreundliche
Hochhaus in Moskau. Bis zu 75 Prozent der Arbeits-
plätze können mit Tageslicht versorgt werden.
Entworfen wurde es von dem New Yorker Büro Frank
Williams & Partners zusammen mit dem Moskauer
Architekten Michail M. Posokhin. Die aus neun
zusätzlichen Stockwerken bestehende Turmspitze wie
auch die luxuriöse Innenarchitektur gehen auf einen
Entwurf des niederländischen Architekten Erick van
Egeraat zurück.

This highrise in the Moscow International Business
Center is strikingly tapered towards the top in a
stepped fashion and is currently the highest
building in Europe as well as the first environmen-
tally friendly building in Moscow. Up to 75 percent
of the workspace can be supplied with daylight. It
was designed by the New York office Frank
Williams & Partners, in collaboration with Moscow-
based architect Michail M. Posokhin. The tip,
which consists of nine additional floors, and the
luxurious interior design are based on plans by the
Dutch architect Erick van Egeraat.

Nominiertes Projekt 2014
Nominated Project 2014

Foster + Partners
THE BOW
Calgary, Kanada **Canada**

Architekten **Architects** Foster + Partners, London
Projektarchitekten **Project architects** Nigel Dancy, Giles Robinson, Nick Ling
Assoziierte Architekten **Associate architects** Zeidler Partnership, Toronto
Bauherr **Client** H + R Real Estate Investment Trust

Höhe **Height** 236 m
Geschosse **Floors** 58
Grundstücksfläche **Site area** 17 500 m²
Bebaute Fläche **Footprint** 3584 m²
Nettogeschossfläche **Net floor area** 199 781 m²
Konstruktion **Structure** Stahlskelett mit Diagridkonstruktion **Steel-braced moment frame with a diagrid**
Fertigstellung **Completion** Januar **January** 2013
Nutzung **Use** Büros, Wohnen, Einzelhandel **Offices, residential and retail**
Ökologische Aspekte / Nachhaltigkeit **Ecological criteria / sustainability** Filigrane Tragwerkskonstruktion; natürliche Belichtung; Speicherung der Sonnenenergie im Atrium. **Filigree load-bearing structure; natural lighting; storage of solar energy in the atrium.**

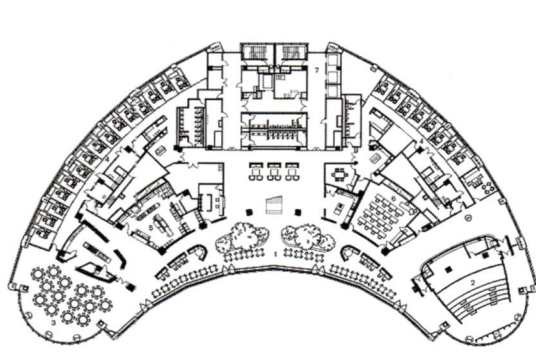

Grundriss 5. Obergeschoss
Floor plan level 5

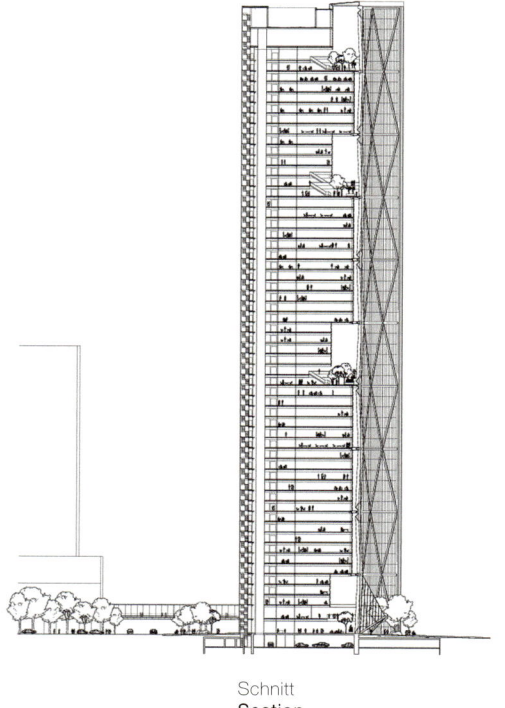

Schnitt
Section

Im Stadtzentrum von Calgary fällt das 58-geschossige Bürohochhaus durch seine gekurvte Form auf. An der konvexen Seite kann das Sonnenlicht in dieser relativ kalten Klimazone über den Tag hinweg optimal genutzt werden. Gleichzeitig werden die starken Windlasten abgefangen, wodurch die Tragwerkskonstruktion weniger aufwendig konzipiert werden musste. Sie basiert auf einem diagonal ausgelegten Metallgitterwerk (diagrid system), das statische Funktionen übernimmt und die Fassade strukturiert. Auf dem 24., 42. und 54. Stockwerk gibt es natürlich bepflanzte „Sky Gardens", die jeweils über sechs Etagen reichen. Sie sorgen für eine natürliche Belichtung der angrenzenden Büro-räume und verbessern das Innenklima.

The striking feature of the 58-storey office highrise in downtown Calgary is its curved shape. On the convex side the sunlight can be used to optimum effect all day long in this relatively cold climate zone. At the same time the strong winds can be headed off, so that the load-bearing structure did not have to be as elaborate. It is based on a diagrid system that takes on load-bearing functions and structures the façade. There are naturally planted 'sky gardens', each six floors high, on floors 24, 42 and 54. They allow the neighbouring offices spaces to enjoy natural light and also improve the building's interior climate.

Nominiertes Projekt 2014
Nominated Project 2014

Gruber + Kleine-Kraneburg Architekten
TAUNUSTURM
Frankfurt am Main, Deutschland **Germany**

Architekten **Architects** Gruber + Kleine-Kraneburg
Architekten, Frankfurt am Main
Assoziierte Architekten **Associate architects**
Planungsgemeinschaft Braun Vollerth, Frankfurt am
Main; Dietz Joppien Architekten, Frankfurt am Main
Bauherr **Client** Tishman Speyer, Commerz Real

Höhe **Height** 170 m
Geschosse **Floors** 40
Grundstücksfläche **Site area** 5527 m²
Bebaute Fläche **Footprint** 3364 m²
Nettogeschossfläche **Net floor area** 60 000 m²
Konstruktion **Structure** Stahlbeton mit vorgefertigten
Betonelementen für Stützen und Bodenplatten
**Reinforced concrete with pre-fab concrete elements
for supports and floor slabs**

Fertigstellung **Completion** Januar **January** 2014
Nutzung **Use** Büros, Museum, Wohnen **Offices,
museum, residential**
Ökologische Aspekte / Nachhaltigkeit **Ecological
criteria / sustainability** Energieeinsparungen bis 30
Prozent durch Hybrid-Heiz- und Kühldeckensysteme;
intelligentes Fassadensystem; optimale Tageslichtnutzung; Blockheizkraftwerk. Nominiert für die
Auszeichnung LEED Platin.
**Energy savings of up to 30 percent thanks to the
hybrid ceiling heating and cooling systems; intelligent
façade system; optimum daylight use; CHP station.
Nominated for the LEED Platinum award.**

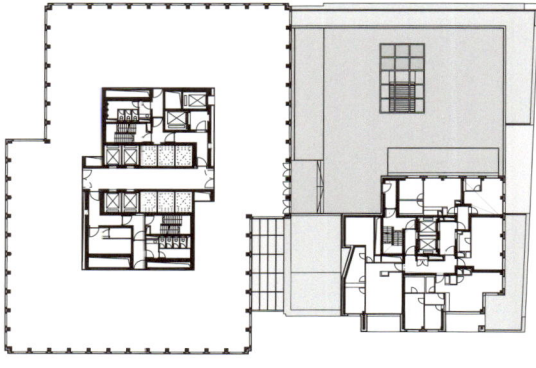

Grundriss 7. Obergeschoss
Floor plan level 7

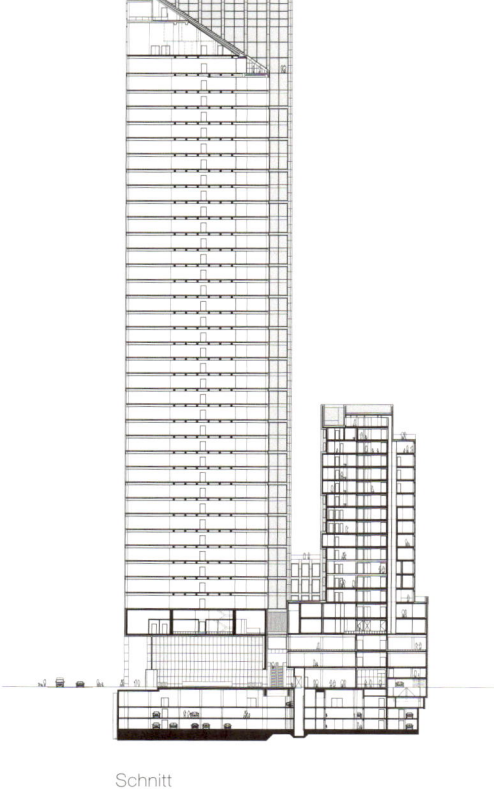

Schnitt
Section

Mit einer Rasterfassade aus weißem Kalkstein und Glas
sowie zwei gegenläufigen Dachabschrägungen wirkt
das Hochhaus skulptural. Sein Grundriss besteht aus
zwei versetzt angeordneten Quadraten, die an der
Kubatur der Fassaden ablesbar bleiben. Im Erdgeschoss öffnet sich ein großzügiges Eingangsfoyer zu
den angrenzenden Wallanlagen. Hier erschließt ein
kleiner öffentlicher Platz die in einem niedrigeren
Gebäudeteil untergebrachten Wohnungen wie auch
eine Dependance des Museums für Moderne Kunst
(MMK).

The highrise has a grid-like façade made of white
limestone and glass, and two contrasting rooflines,
both of which give it a sculptural feel. Its floor plan
consists of two offset squares that are reflected
elsewhere in the design, such as the cube-like nature
of the façades. A generous foyer on the ground floor
opens up to the neighbouring green space with
earthworks. A small public square gives access to a
lower section of the building, which houses flats as
well as a branch of the Museum für Moderne Kunst
(MMK).

Nominiertes Projekt 2014
Nominated Project 2014

MAD Architects
SHERATON HUZHOU HOT SPRING RESORT
Huzhou, China

Architekten **Architects** MAD Architects, Peking **Beijing**
Assoziierte Architekten **Associate architects** Shanghai
Sian Dai Architecture Design (Group) Co. Ltd.
Bauherr **Client** Feizhou Group

Höhe **Height** 102 m
Geschosse **Floors** 27
Grundstücksfläche **Site area** 5566 m²
Bebaute Fläche **Footprint** 2400 m²
Nettogeschossfläche **Net floor area** 59 686 m²
Konstruktion **Structure** Stahlbeton **Reinforced concrete**
Fertigstellung **Completion** Dezember **December** 2012
Nutzung **Use** Hotel

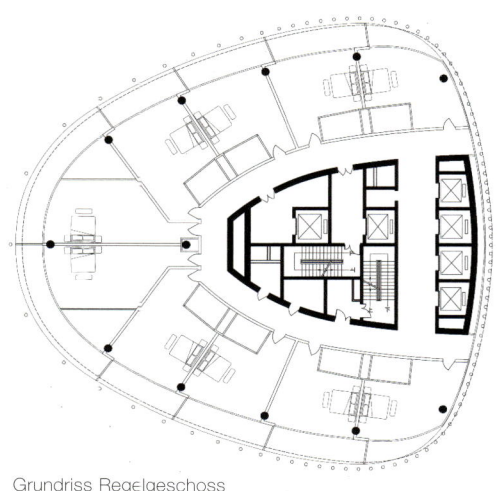

Grundriss Regelgeschoss
Typical floor plan

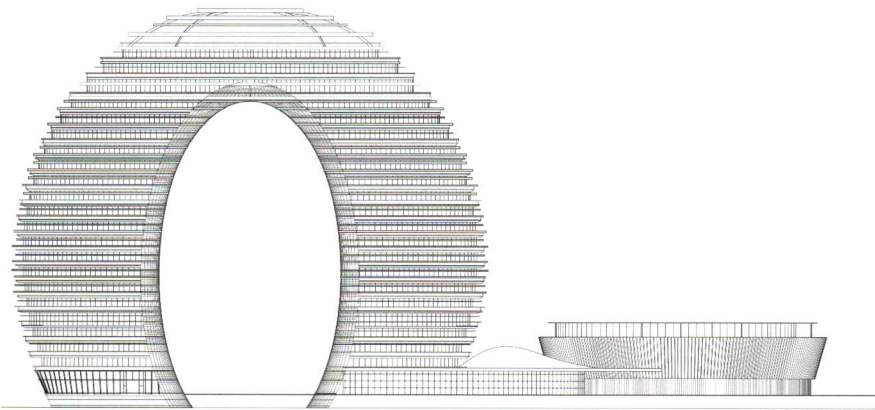

Nordostansicht
Elevation north-east

Wie ein organisch geformter großer Ring liegt das
Hochhaus am Taihu-See bei Huzhou. Zusammen mit
seiner Spiegelung im Wasser vervollständigt sich seine
Silhouette zu einer Acht. Nicht nur der Name des 27
Stockwerke zählenden „Sheraton Moon Hotel‚ weist
auf eine genuin chinesische Konzeption hin, sondern
auch sein Ansatz, Architektur und Natur in harmonisch
fließenden Formen miteinander zu verbinden.

This highrise in the shape of a large 'O' is located on
the banks of Lake Taihu near Huzhou. Its reflection on
the water completes its silhouette to look like a figure
'8'. It is not just the name of the 27-storey 'Sheraton
Moon Hotel' that indicates its genuinely Chinese
design. Other pointers include the approach of
combining architecture and nature in harmoniously
flowing forms.

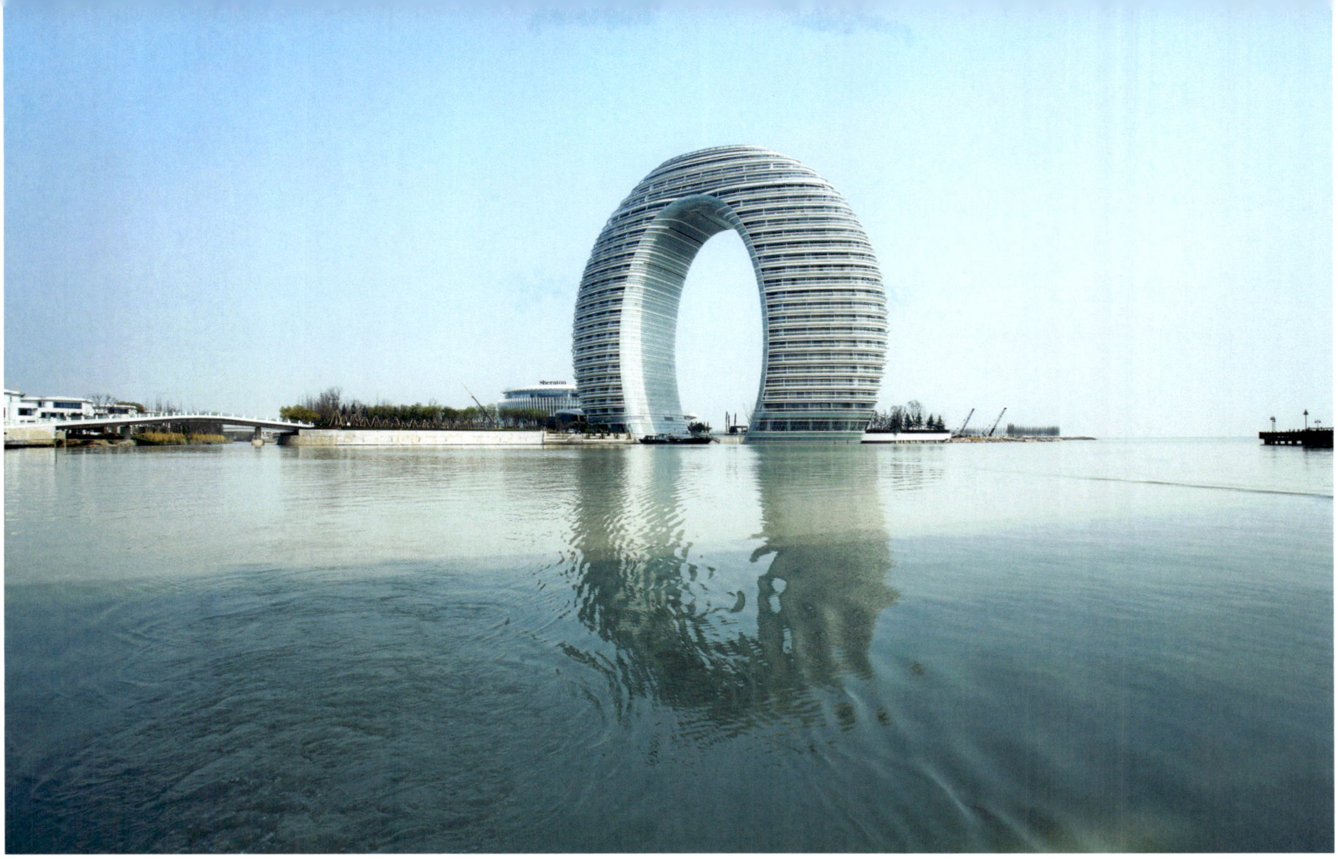

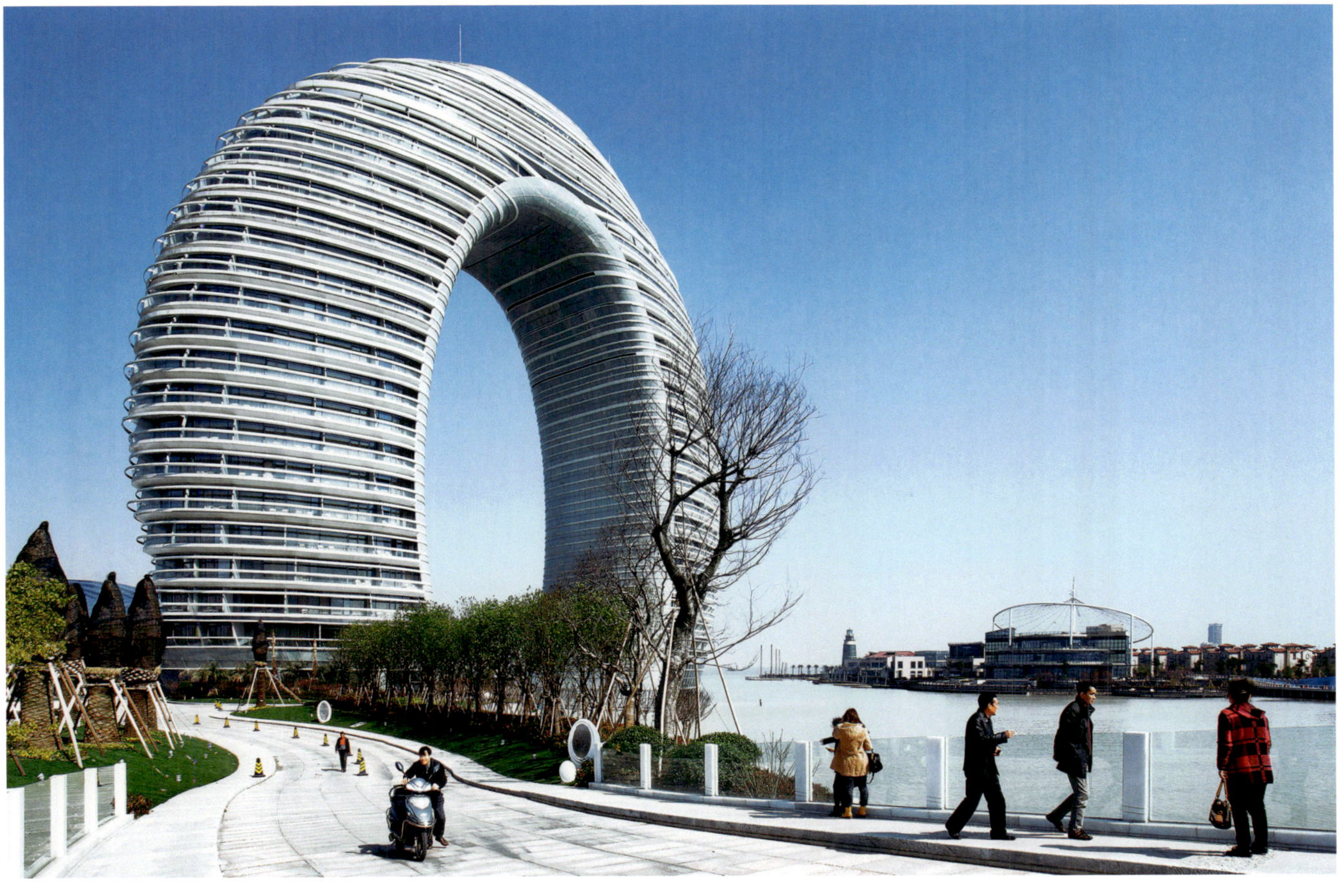

Nominiertes Projekt 2014
Nominated Project 2014

Prof. Christoph Mäckler Architekten
ZOOFENSTER – WALDORF ASTORIA BERLIN
Berlin, Deutschland **Germany**

Architekten **Architects** Prof. Christoph Mäckler
Architekten, Frankfurt am Main
Bauherr **Client** Harvest United Enterprises

Höhe **Height** 119 m
Geschosse **Floors** 32
Grundstücksfläche **Site area** 2870 m²

Bebaute Fläche **Footprint** 2839 m²
Nettogeschossfläche **Net floor area** 26 846 m²
Konstruktion **Structure** Beton, Stahl **Concrete, steel**
Fertigstellung **Completion** November 2012
Nutzung **Use** Hotel, Büros, Cafés, Einzelhandel **Hotel,
offices, cafes, shops**
Ökologische Aspekte / Nachhaltigkeit **Ecological
criteria / sustainability** Steinfassade mit nur 50 Prozent
Öffnungen sorgt für optimale Dämmung und
Dauerhaftigkeit; Solarverglasung; Blockheizkraftwerk.
**Stone façade with just 50 percent openings ensures
optimum insulation and durability; solar glazing; CHP
station.**

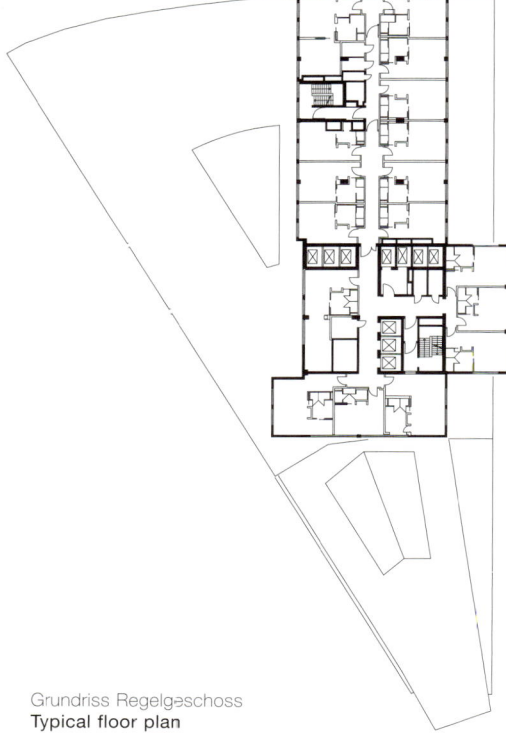

Grundriss Regelgeschoss
Typical floor plan

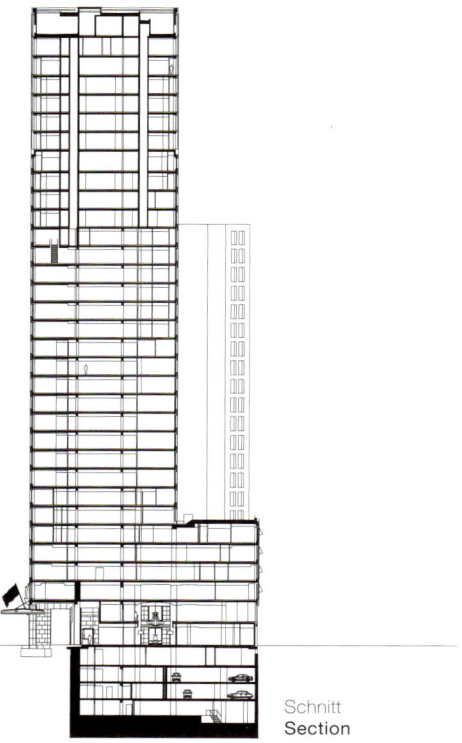

Schnitt
Section

In seiner Grundform nimmt das Hochhaus den
Straßenverlauf zum Breitscheidplatz hin auf und staffelt
sich von einer Blockrandbebauung auf 22 und schließlich auf 32 Stockwerke hoch. Der Gebäudekomplex
ist mit Naturstein verkleidet. An seiner Spitze ist der
Turm großflächig verglast und tritt mit einem „Fenster
zum Zoo" in einen Dialog zum benachbarten Tierpark
und dem gegenüberliegenden Europacenter.

The basic shape of the highrise reflects the street
layout to Breitscheidplatz; it is a block perimeter
development which rises in steps to 22 floors and
finally 32 floors. The building is clad in natural stone. At
the top of the tower generous use was made of
glazing. This 'window to the zoo' allows the building to
engage in a dialogue with the neighbouring zoological
gardens and the Europa Center opposite.

Nominiertes Projekt 2014
Nominated Project 2014

Ateliers Jean Nouvel
DOHA TOWER
Doha, Katar **Qatar**

Architekten **Architects** Ateliers Jean Nouvel, Paris
Bauherr **Client** H.E. Sheikh Saud Al-Thani

Höhe **Height** 231 m
Geschosse **Floors** 46
Grundstücksfläche **Site area** 13 000 m²
Bebaute Fläche **Footprint** 2240 m²
Nettogeschossfläche **Net floor area** 60 000 m²
Konstruktion **Structure** Stahl, Beton **Steel, concrete**
Fertigstellung **Completion** April 2012
Nutzung **Use** Büros, Gästehaus, Restaurant **Offices, hotel, restaurant**

Ökologische Aspekte / Nachhaltigkeit **Ecological criteria / sustainability** Doppelfassade mit außen liegendem Verschattungssystem aus Aluminium-elementen, die je nach Himmelsrichtung unterschied-lich gestaltet sind; innen liegende Sonnenschutz-fassade mit Jalousien.
Double façade with an external shading system made of aluminium elements that feature different designs depending on the direction they are facing; internal sun protection façade with blinds.

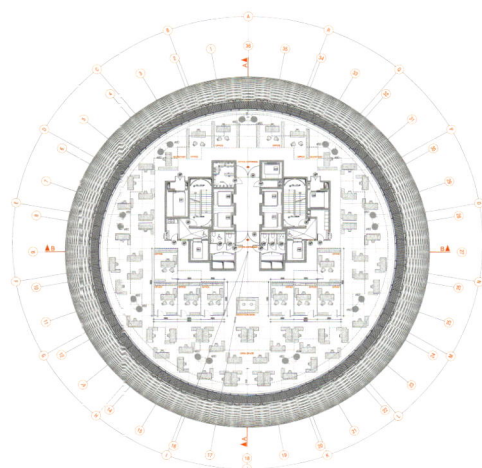

Grundriss Regelgeschoss Büros
Typical floor plan offices

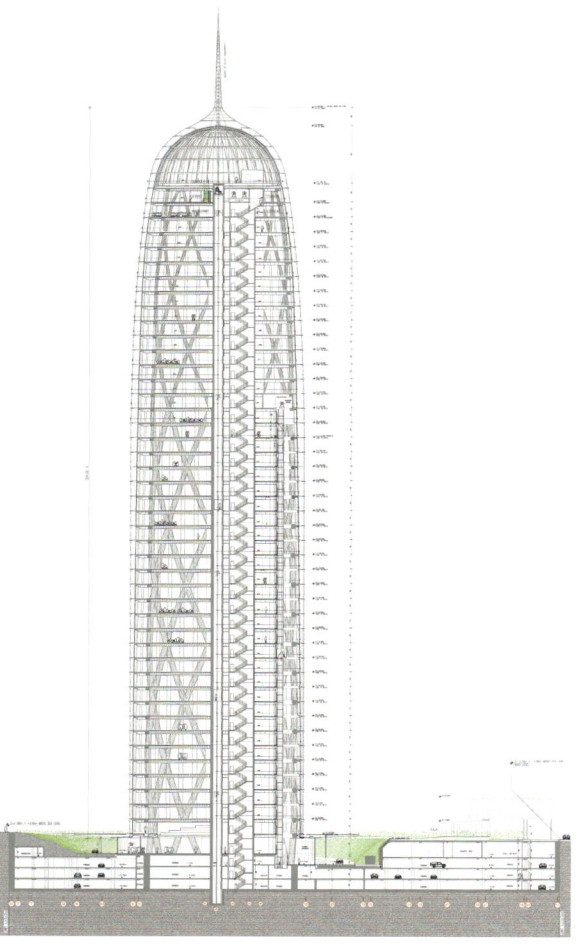

Schnitt
Section

Am Golf von Doha setzt das 46-stöckige Büro- und Hotelgebäude mit einer zylindrisch anschwellenden und in einer flachen Kuppel abschließenden Form einen markanten Akzent. Im Inneren reicht ein Atrium bis zur 27. Etage. In seinem äußeren Erscheinungsbild ist das Hochhaus eine Weiterentwicklung des von Nouvel 2004 in Barcelona erbauten Torre Agbar. Die aus filigranen Verschattungselementen bestehende Fassade leitet sich vom Institut du Monde Arabe in Paris ab, das Nouvel 1987 realisierte.

The 46-storey office and hotel building on Doha Bay is a striking feature with its cylindrical shape that tapers to a shallow dome at the top. Inside, the atrium rises up to the 27th floor. In terms of its appearance, the highrise is a further development of the Torre Agbar built by Nouvel in Barcelona in 2004. The façade, which consists of filigree shading elements, is based on the Institut du Monde Arabe in Paris, which Nouvel implemented in 1987.

Nominiertes Projekt 2014
Nominated Project 2014

Office for Metropolitan Architecture
CCTV HEADQUARTERS
Peking **Beijing**, China

Architekten **Architects** OMA Office for Metropolitan
Architecture Rem Koolhaas and Ole Scheeren,
Rotterdam / Peking **Beijing**
Lokale Architekten **Architects of record** ECADI (East
China Architecture and Design Institute)
Bauherr **Client** China Central Television (CCTV)

Höhe **Height** 234 m
Geschosse **Floors** 54
Grundstücksfläche **Site area** 200 000 m²
Bebaute Fläche **Footprint** 25 600 m²
Nettogeschossfläche **Net floor area** 473 000 m²

Konstruktion **Structure** Kompositstützen, Stahlträger
und Stahlaussteifung **Composite columns, steel beams
and steal supports**
Fertigstellung **Completion** Mai **May** 2012
Nutzung **Use** Verwaltung, Fernseh- und Produktions-
studios **Administration, television and production
studios**
Ökologische Aspekte / Nachhaltigkeit **Ecological
criteria / sustainability** Die Zusammenlegung aller
Bereiche des Senders in einem Gebäude erspart lange
Wege zwischen verschiedenen Produktions- und
Verwaltungsstandorten (Verkehr, Transport);
Reduzierung des Stahlverbrauchs um 20 Prozent im
Vergleich zu einem konventionellen Hochhaus.
**Putting all of the aspects of the broadcaster in one
building saves long journeys between different
production and administration sites (traffic, transport);
reduced steel use by 20 percent compared to
conventional highrises.**

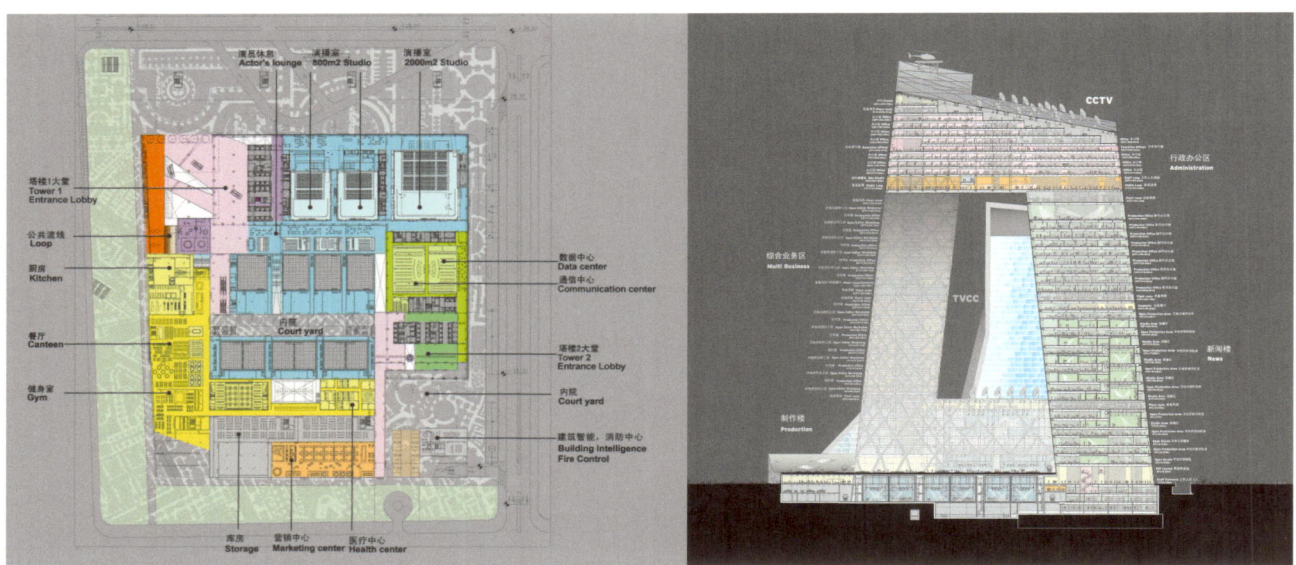

Grundriss Erdgeschoss
Ground floor plan

Schnitt
Section

Das ikonenhafte Bauwerk des staatlichen chinesischen
Fernsehsenders ist in der Skyline Pekings unüber-
sehbar. Mit einer immensen Nutzfläche von 473 000
Quadratmetern ist es nach dem Pentagon in
Washington das zweitgrößte Bürogebäude der Welt.
Die Stahlkonstruktion seines übergreifenden Bügels
beeindruckt als statische Leistung. In seiner
symbolischen Bildwirkung lässt es an eine Endlos-
schleife denken, in der die verschiedenen Aktivitäten
des Senders, die hier zusammengeführt wurden,
kontinuierlich ablaufen.

The iconic headquarters of China's state television
broadcaster is a dominant feature of Beijing's skyline.
With a vast floor space of 473,000 square metres,
it is the second-largest office building in the world,
after the Pentagon in Washington. The steel
construction of its frame is an impressive structural
feat. Its appearance could be taken to symbolize an
infinite loop in which the different activities of the
broadcaster that have been brought together here take
place continuously.

Nominiertes Projekt 2014
Nominated Project 2014

Pelli Clarke Pelli Architects
TORRE COSTANERA
Santiago, Chile

Architekten **Architects** Pelli Clarke Pelli Architects, New Haven, USA
Bauherr **Client** Cencosud S.A.

Höhe **Height** 300 m
Geschosse **Floors** 64
Nettogeschossfläche **Net floor area** 110 000 m²
Konstruktion **Structure** Betonkern mit Betonstützen, in der Turmspitze Stahlträgersystem **Concrete core with concrete supports, a steel beam system in the tip of the tower**

Fertigstellung **Completion** 2014
Nutzung **Use** Büros **Offices**
Ökologische Aspekte / Nachhaltigkeit **Ecological criteria / sustainability** Intelligentes Fassadensystem; Doppeldeckeraufzüge als effizientes Transportsystem. **Intelligent façade system; double-decker elevators as an efficient transport system.**

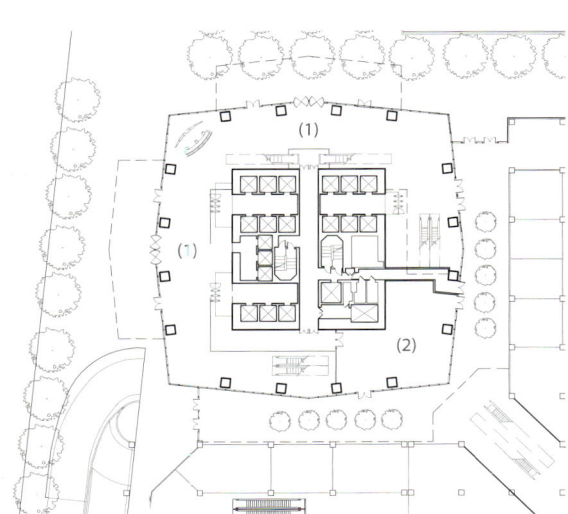

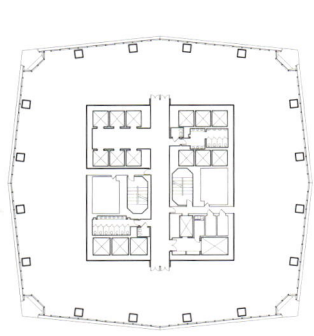

Grundrisse Erd- und Regelgeschoss
Plan ground floor and typical floor plan

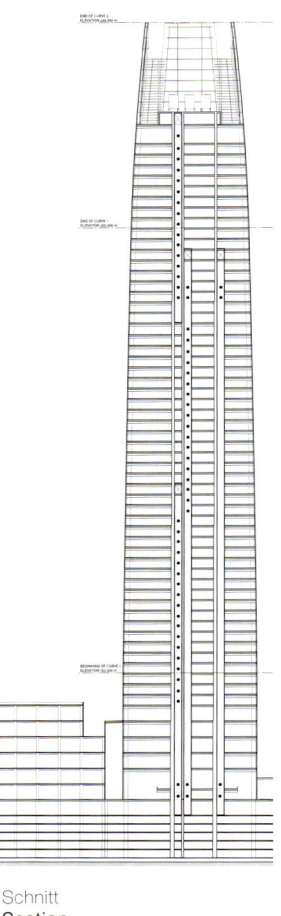

Schnitt
Section

Mit seinen 300 Metern Höhe ist der Torre Costanera das höchste Gebäude Südamerikas. Wie ein schlanker Pfahl vor dem Andenmassiv scheint er nur noch mit dessen höchsten Gipfeln zu konkurrieren. Er ist erdbebensicher konstruiert und seine Fassade übernimmt statische Funktionen. In den oberen Etagen scheint sich die metallene Außenhaut gleich einer Knospe zu öffnen, wodurch die Profilierung besonders dünn und filigran wirkt.

At 300 metres, the Torre Costanera is South America's tallest building. Standing as a narrow pillar in front of the Andean massif, it seems to compete only with the latter's highest peaks. It is earthquake proof and its façade has load-bearing functions. On the top floors the exterior metal skin seems to open itself like a bud, which makes its profile seem particularly slender and delicate.

Dominique Perrault Architecture
DC TOWER I
Wien **Vienna**, Österreich **Austria**

Architekten **Architects** Dominique Perrault Architecture, Paris
Lokale Architekten **Architects of record** Franz Janz (Hofmann-Janz ZT GmbH), Wien **Vienna**
Bauherr **Client** WED Wiener Entwicklungsgesellschaft für den Donauraum

Höhe **Height** 250 m
Geschosse **Floors** 60
Grundstücksfläche **Site area** 11 000 m²
Bebaute Fläche **Footprint** 1596 m²
Nettogeschossfläche **Net floor area** 90 000 m²
Konstruktion **Structure** Stahlbeton **Reinforced concrete**
Fertigstellung **Completion** Februar **February** 2014
Nutzung **Use** Büros, Wohnen, Hotel, Einzelhandel, Restaurants **Offices, residential, hotel, shops and restaurants**

Ökologische Aspekte / Nachhaltigkeit **Ecological criteria / sustainability** Zu öffnende Fenster in allen Büros; Vorhangfassade als Dreifachverglasung zur Optimierung des Sonnenschutzes; Nutzung aufbereiteten Wassers aus der Donau; Photovoltaik; Sonnensegel zur Abwehr der Fallwinde in den Außenbereichen. Nominiert für die Auszeichnung LEED Gold.
Windows that can be opened in all of the offices; curtain wall, triple-glazed to provide the best-possible solar protection; use of treated water from the Danube; photovoltaic system; sun sails to deal with fall winds affecting the exterior. Nominated for the LEED Gold award.

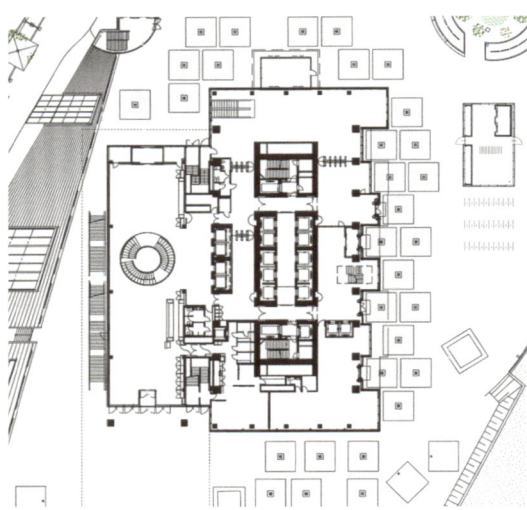

Grundriss Erdgeschoss
Ground floor plan

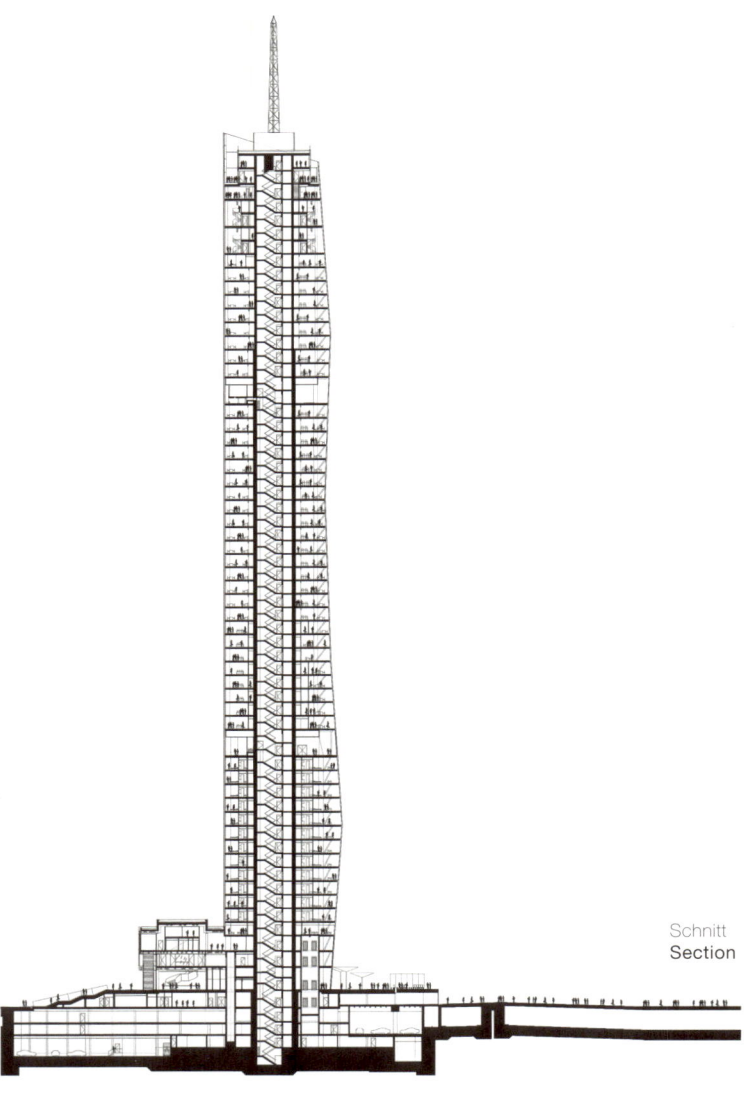

Schnitt
Section

Der DC Tower ist der erste von ursprünglich zwei Türmen, die eindrucksvoll das Tor zur Wiener Donaucity bilden sollten. Er steht im rechten Winkel zum Fluss und wirkt aufgrund seiner äußerst schmalen Abmessungen von nur 28 x 59 Metern extrem schlank. Seine durchgehende Verkleidung aus schwarzem Glas legt sich an der Südseite in Falten und verleiht dem Turm etwas reflektierend Schillerndes.

The DC Tower I is the first of what was originally to be two towers that were meant to form an impressive gateway to Vienna's Donau City. It stands perpendicular to the river and because of its extremely narrow dimensions of just 28 x 59 metres, it appears incredibly slender. Its all-over black glass cladding has been given a relief structure on the southern elevation, giving the tower a reflective, shimmering air.

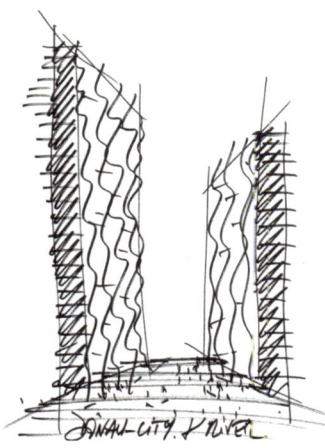

Nominiertes Projekt 2014
Nominated Project 2014

Renzo Piano Building Workshop
THE SHARD LONDON BRIDGE TOWER
London, Großbritannien **UK**

Architekten **Architects** Renzo Piano Building Workshop,
Paris
Bauherr **Client** Sellar Property Group

Höhe **Height** 310 m
Geschosse **Floors** 72
Grundstücksfläche **Site area** 4461 m²
Bebaute Fläche **Footprint** 4461 m²
Nettogeschossfläche **Net floor area** 83 104 m²
Konstruktion **Structure** Stahl, Beton, Glas **Steel,
concrete, glass**

Fertigstellung **Completion** Juli **July** 2012
Nutzung **Use** Wohnen, Gewerbe, Einzelhandel
Residential, commercial, retail
Ökologische Aspekte / Nachhaltigkeit **Ecological
criteria / sustainability** Nachhaltige Stadtentwicklung mit
Verdichtungen an Verkehrsknotenpunkten; Doppelver-
glasung mit integrierten Jalousien ermöglicht natürliche
Belüftung und Verschattung.
**Sustainable urban development with densification at
central transport hubs; double glazing with integrated
blinds for natural ventilation and shading.**

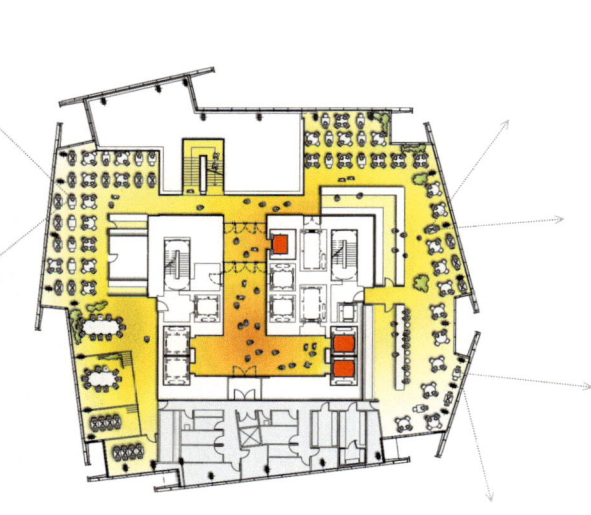

Grundriss 39. Obergeschoss
Floor plan level 39

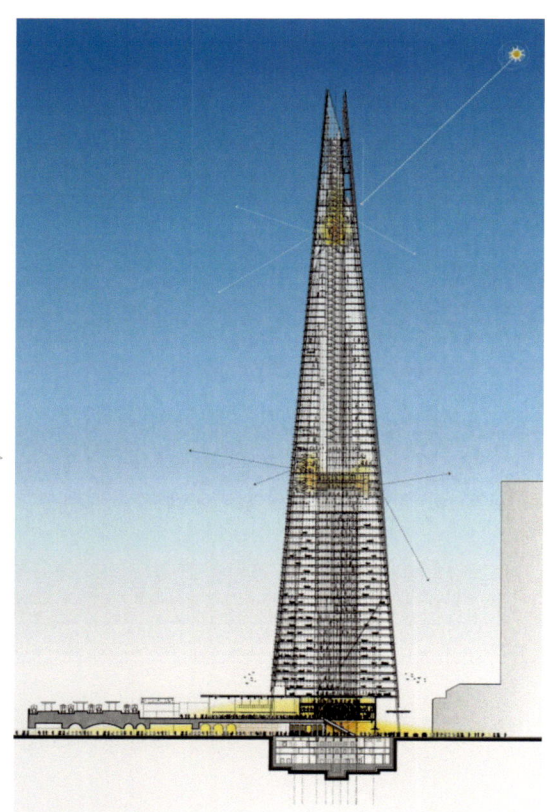

Schnitt
Section

Mit seiner filigranen Glas-Stahl-Konstruktion setzt „The
Shard" einen neuen Akzent im historischen London-
Bridge-Quartier. Der Turm verjüngt sich pyramidal nach
oben und scheint sich dort fast aufzulösen. Seine acht
unterschiedlich geneigten Fassaden bestehen aus
einer doppelschaligen Verglasung mit innen liegender
Verschattungstechnik. Wintergärten auf verschiedenen
Etagen können dadurch natürlich belüftet werden. In
den unteren Ebenen sind Mischnutzungen angesiedelt,
darüber Wohnungen bis in die oberen Stockwerke
sowie eine Aussichtsplattform in 240 Meter Höhe.

With its filigree glass and steel construction, 'The
Shard' has created a new focus in the historic London
Bridge quarter. The tower tapers to the top in a
pyramid-like fashion, where it then seems to almost
disappear. Its eight façades, all with different
inclinations, consist of double glazing with integrated
shading technology. Conservatories on various floors
can therefore be ventilated naturally. The lower floors
are mixed use, while the floors above, all the way to
the top, are given over to residences. There is a
viewing platform at 240 metres.

Nominiertes Projekt 2014
Nominated Project 2014

Atelier Christian de Portzamparc
ONE 57
New York City, USA

Architekten **Architects** Atelier Christian de Portzamparc, Paris
Assoziierte Architekten **Associate architects** Handel Architects LLP, New York
Bauherr **Client** Extell Development Company

Höhe **Height** 306 m
Geschosse **Floors** 75
Grundstücksfläche **Site area** 2211 m²
Bebaute Fläche **Footprint** 2071 m²
Nettogeschossfläche **Net floor area** 74 350 m²
Konstruktion **Structure** Stahlbeton **Reinforced concrete**
Fertigstellung **Completion** 2014
Nutzung **Use** Hotel, Wohnen **Hotel, residential**

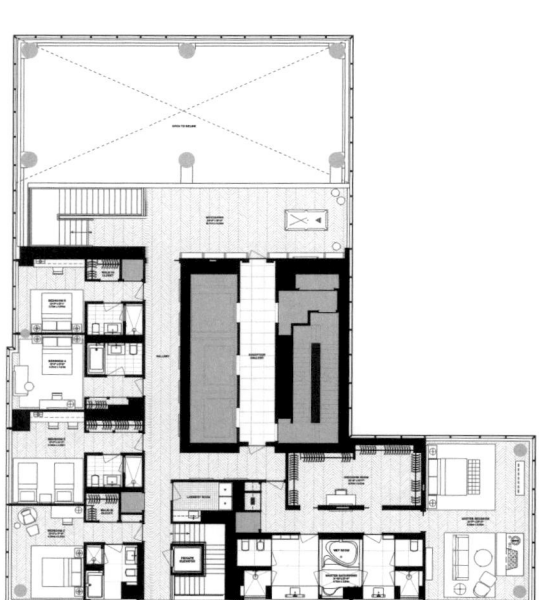

Grundriss Mustergeschoss
Floor plan of sample storey

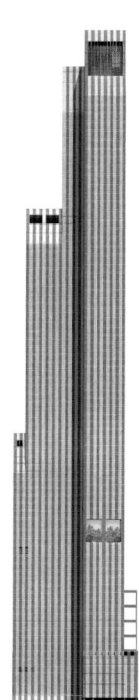 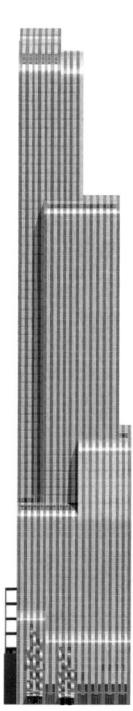 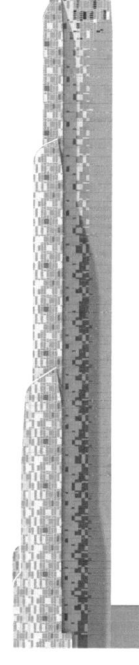

Süd-, Nord- und Ostansichten
Elevations: south, north and east

Der aufgrund der engen Grundstücksbemessungen in Manhattan extrem schlanke Turm ist mit 306 Metern das höchste Wohnhochhaus New Yorks. Seine durchgehende Verglasung ist an allen Seiten unterschiedlich abgetreppt. Das Motiv der Kaskade dient als ein Leitbild, das sich am schönsten an der Straßenfassade des Eingangsbereichs zeigt, wo gläserne Ein- und Auswölbungen ein Fließen suggerieren.

This tower in Manhattan is extremely slim because of its tight footprint, but at 306 metres it is the tallest residential building in New York. Its all-over glass façade is stepped in different intervals on all sides. The model was the cascade motif; it can be best seen on the street front where the entrance is located; the glass ripples create a flowing effect.

Nominiertes Projekt 2014
Nominated Project 2014

Rapp und Rapp
DE KROON
Den Haag **The Hague**, Niederlande **Netherlands**

Architekten **Architects** Rapp und Rapp, Amsterdam
Bauherr **Client** Wijnhavenkwartier Ontwikkeling Fase I CV

Höhe **Height** 131 m
Geschosse **Floors** 40
Grundstücksfläche **Site area** 3400 m²
Bebaute Fläche **Footprint** 3350 m²
Nettogeschossfläche **Net floor area** 50 000 m²
Konstruktion **Structure** Stahlbeton **Reinforced concrete**
Fertigstellung **Completion** Juli **July** 2011
Nutzung **Use** Büros und Wohnen **Offices and residential**

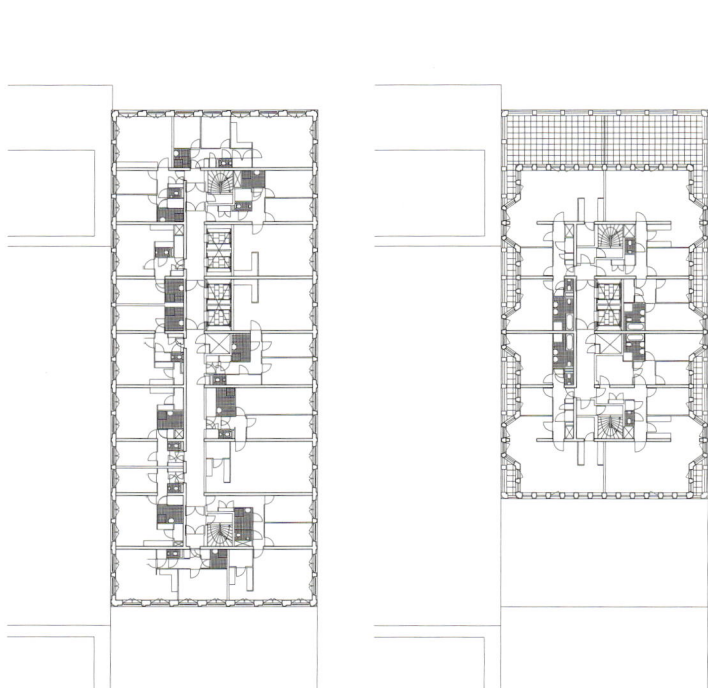

Grundrisse 9. und 17. Obergeschoss
Floor plan level 9 and 17

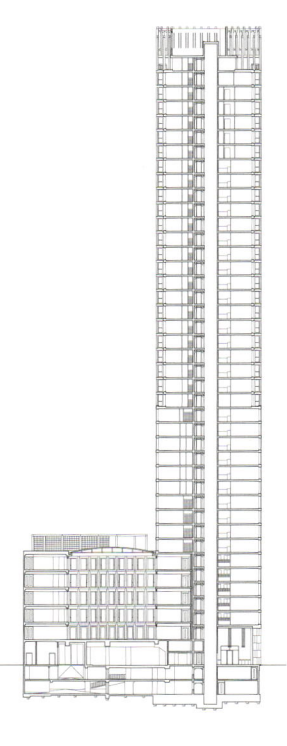

Schnitt
Section

Das Büro- und Wohnhochhaus setzt einen wuchtigen Akzent im Regierungsviertel von Den Haag. Der bei Hans Kollhoff in Berlin ausgebildete Christian Rapp suchte seine Vorbilder im frühen Hochhausbau in Chicago und New York. Der kompakte Gebäudeblock stuft sich nach oben bis zu einem 131 Meter hohen Turm, dessen aus Beton und Naturstein kombinierte Fassade durch Erkerfenster strukturiert wird.

This office and residential highrise has set a powerful mark in The Hague's government district. Christian Rapp, who trained with Hans Kollhoff in Berlin, found his inspiration in the early highrises of Chicago and New York. The compact building complex narrows in steps, to an ultimate height of 131 metres; its façade, made of concrete and natural stone, is structured by its oriel windows.

Nominiertes Projekt 2014
Nominated Project 2014

Rogers Stirk Harbour + Partners
8 CHIFLEY SQUARE
Sydney, Australien **Australia**

Architekten **Architects** Rogers Stirk Harbour and
Partners, London
Lokale Architekten **Architects of record** Lippmann
Partnership, Sydney
Bauherr **Client** Mirac Developments

Höhe **Height** 110 m
Geschosse **Floors** 30
Grundstücksfläche **Site area** 1580 m²
Bebaute Fläche **Footprint** 1200 m²
Nettogeschossfläche **Net floor area** 19 000 m²
Konstruktion **Structure** Nachversteifte Betonplatten mit
vorgefertigten Stahlbetonstützen, stahlummanteltes
Betontragwerk, Querversteifungen **Strutted concrete
slabs with prefab reinforced concrete supports;
steel-clad concrete structure; cross-bracing**
Fertigstellung **Completion** Juli **July** 2013
Nutzung **Use** Büros **Offices**

Ökologische Aspekte / Nachhaltigkeit **Ecological
criteria / sustainability** Externe Sonnenschutz-
vorrichtungen an Nordost- und Westfassade; chilled
beams (Klimatechnik); um 50 Prozent reduzierte
Kohlenstoffemission; reduzierter Wasserverbrauch;
Verwendung nachhaltiger Materialien. Auszeichnung
Australian Green Star 6 Sterne.
**External solar-protection measures on the northeast
and west elevations; chilled beams (HVAC technology);
carbon emissions reduced by up to 50 percent;
reduced water usage; use of sustainable materials.
Awarded Australian Green Star 6 stars.**

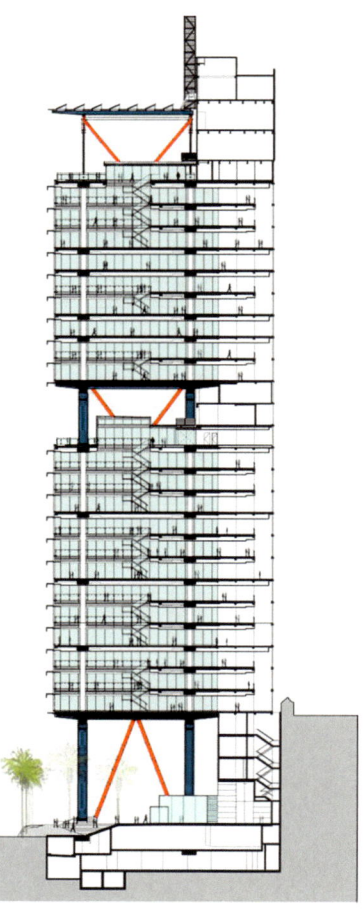

Schnitt
Section

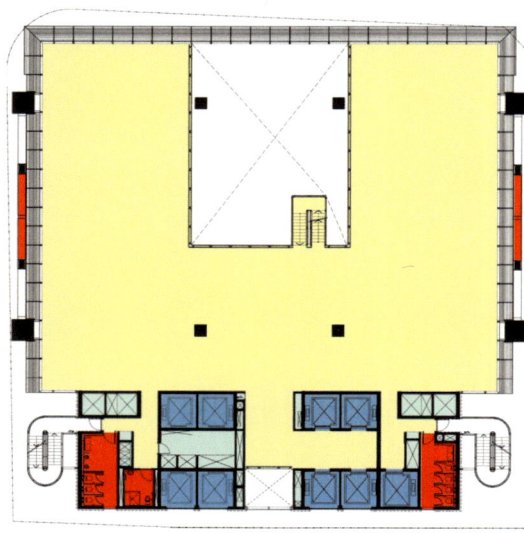

Grundriss Regelgeschoss
Typical floor plan

Die für Richard Rogers typische Verlagerung tech-
nischer Funktionen nach außen lässt die Büroetagen
an mächtigen externen Stützen aufgehängt erscheinen,
die ihrerseits wiederum von querversteifenden, rot
gefassten Stahlträgern zusammengehalten werden. Auf
Bodenniveau ist das Gebäude um fünf Etagen
angehoben, sodass hier ein öffentlicher Platz entsteht.
Im 18. Geschoss ergab sich durch die Aussparung
von drei Etagen ein weiterer Freiraum für die
Angestellten.

The relocation of engineering functions to the outside,
a move typical of Richard Rogers, makes the office
floors appear as if they are hanging from massive
external supports, which are in turn held together by
the cross-bracing of red-painted steel supports. On
the ground level, the building has been raised from the
ground by five floors to create a public square beneath
it. On the 18th floor, three further floors were cut out,
creating a further open space for the employees.

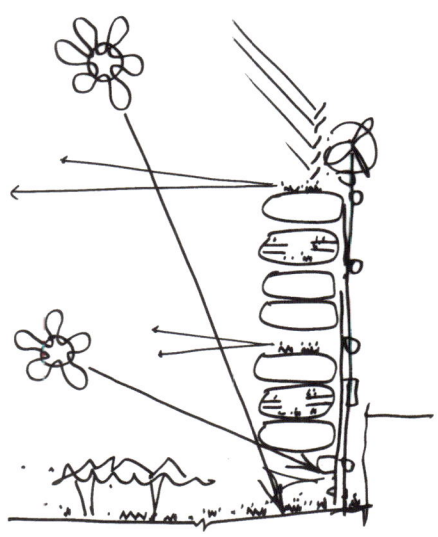

Skizze **Sketch**

Nominiertes Projekt 2014
Nominated Project 2014

Rogers Stirk Harbour + Partners
THE LEADENHALL BUILDING
London, Großbritannien **UK**

Architekten **Architects** Rogers Stirk Harbour + Partners, London
Bauherr **Client** The British Land Company plc + Oxford Properties

Höhe **Height** 224 m
Geschosse **Floors** 50
Grundstücksfläche **Site area** 3500 m²
Bebaute Fläche **Footprint** 3500 m²
Nettogeschossfläche **Net floor area** 58 000 m²
Konstruktion **Structure** Stahl **Steel**
Fertigstellung **Completion** September 2014
Nutzung **Use** Büros **Offices**
Ökologische Aspekte / Nachhaltigkeit **Ecological criteria / sustainability** Optimale Tageslichtnutzung durch geschosshohe Verglasung an der Süd-, Ost- und Westfassade.
Optimum use of daylight thanks to floor-to-ceiling windows on the south, east and west elevations.

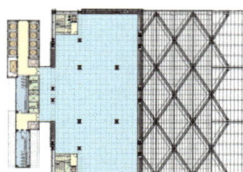
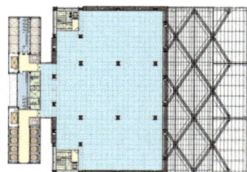
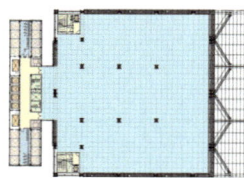

Grundriss 5., 22. und 31. Obergeschoss
Floor plans level 5, 22 and 31

Schnitt
Section

Aufgrund einer geforderten Blickachse zur St. Pauls Kathedrale verjüngt sich das Hochhaus in seinen oberen Stockwerken extrem. Alle vertikalen Funktionen des Stahlträgerbaus sind in einen separaten Turm an der Nordseite ausgelagert, der zugleich der Stabilisierung des Hauptgebäudes dient. Dessen Erdgeschoss ist mit einem 30 Meter hohen Atrium öffentlich zugänglich und bietet einen Durchgang zum nahegelegenen St. Helens Park.

Thanks to the protected view of St Paul's Cathedral, the highrise tapers dramatically towards the top. All of the vertical functions of the steel beam structure have been moved to a separate tower on the north elevation; this tower also acts as a stabilizer for the main building. Its ground floor with its 30-metre-high atrium is open to the public and provides a walk-through to nearby St Helen's Park.

Nominiertes Projekt 2014
Nominated Project 2014

Skidmore, Owings and Merrill LLP
CAYAN TOWER
Dubai, Vereinigte Arabische Emirate **United Arab Emirates**

Architekten **Architects** Skidmore, Owings and Merrill LLP, Chicago
Bauherr **Client** Cayan Investment and Development

Höhe **Height** 307 m
Geschosse **Floors** 75
Grundstücksfläche **Site area** 3027 m²
Bebaute Fläche **Footprint** 2928 m²
Nettogeschossfläche **Net floor area** 110 000 m²
Konstruktion **Structure** Stahlbeton **Reinforced concrete**
Fertigstellung **Completion** Juni **June** 2013
Nutzung **Use** Wohnen **Residential**
Ökologische Aspekte / Nachhaltigkeit **Ecological criteria / sustainability** Tief eingeschnittene Fensterlaibungen und Balkone zur Verringerung direkter Sonnenlichteinstrahlung.
Deep window bays and balconies to reduce the amount of direct sunlight entering the building.

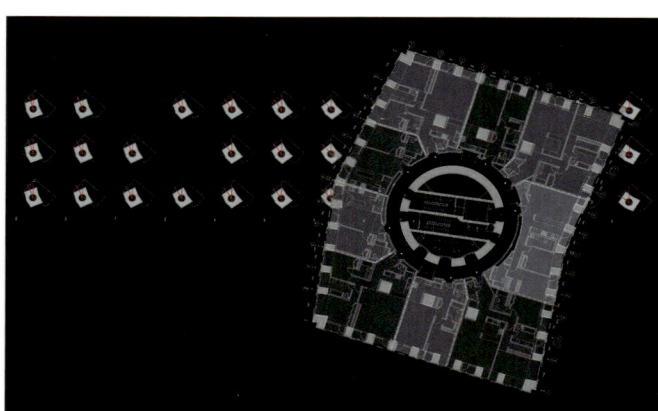

Grundriss Regelgeschoss
Typical floor plan

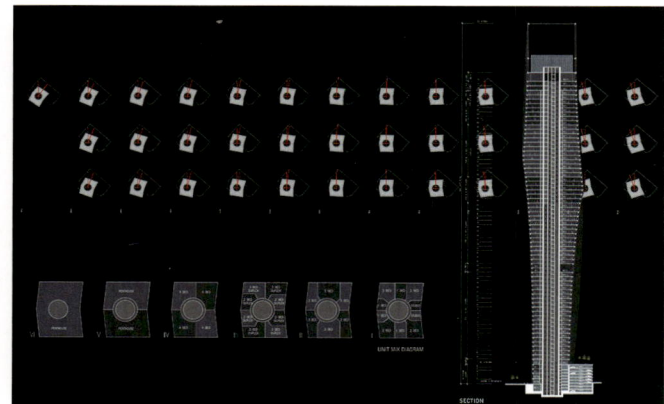

Geschossvarianten und Schnitt
Storey variations and cutaway

In der heterogenen Skyline am Golf von Dubai fällt der neue Wohnturm durch seine helixartig gedrehte Form auf. Er umfasst 495 Luxuswohneinheiten. Seine Konstruktion basiert auf einem Gebäudekern, um den die 75 Stockwerksplatten jeweils um 1,2° versetzt angeordnet sind, sodass sich eine Gesamtdrehung von 90° ergibt.

The new residential highrise stands out from the heterogeneous skyline on the Gulf thanks to its helically twisted shape. It contains 495 luxury flats. Its construction is based on a core around which each of the 75 floor slabs has been shifted by 1.2° relative to the one below, creating a total twist of 90°.

Nominiertes Projekt 2014
Nominated Project 2014

Skidmore, Owings and Merrill LLP
PEARL RIVER TOWER
Guangzhou, China

Architekten **Architects** Skidmore, Owings and Merrill
LLP, Chicago
Lokale Architekten **Architects of record** Guangzhou
Design Institute, Guangzhou
Bauherr **Client** The Guangzhou Pearl River Tower
Properties Co. Ltd.

Höhe **Height** 309 m
Geschosse **Floors** 71
Grundstücksfläche **Site area** 10 635 m²
Bebaute Fläche **Footprint** 5741 m²
Nettogeschossfläche **Net floor area** 214 000 m²
Konstruktion **Structure** Betonkern mit Stahlrahmen und
intelligenter Glasfassade **Concrete core with steel
frame and high performance glass-façade system**
Fertigstellung **Completion** April 2013
Nutzung **Use** Büros **Offices**

Ökologische Aspekte / Nachhaltigkeit **Ecological
criteria / sustainability** Durch die konvexe Form hält das
Gebäude Windlasten stand und ermöglicht eine
weniger massive Tragwerkkonstruktion; Entlastung des
öffentlichen Stromnetzes durch Eigenproduktion von
Energie; reduzierte Kohlenstoffemission; um 44 Prozent
reduzierter Energiebedarf; Windturbinen (Vertical Axis
Wind Turbines VAWT); Photovoltaik; Tageslichtreflektoren; Doppeldeckeraufzüge; effiziente Kühlungs- und
Belichtungssysteme. Nominiert für die Auszeichnung
LEED Platin.
The convex shape allows the building to withstand
strong winds and makes it possible to make do with a
less massive load-bearing construction; the public
electricity grid is relieved because the tower produces
its own energy; reduced carbon emissions; 44 percent
reduced energy needs; wind turbines (Vertical Axis
Wind Turbines VAWT); photovoltaic system; daylight
reflectors; double-decker elevators; efficient cooling
and lighting systems. Nominated for the LEED Platinum
award.

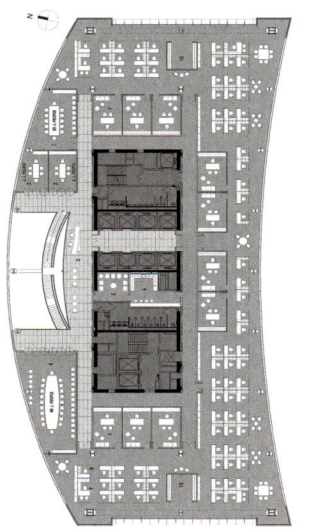

Grundriss Regelgeschoss
Typical floor plan

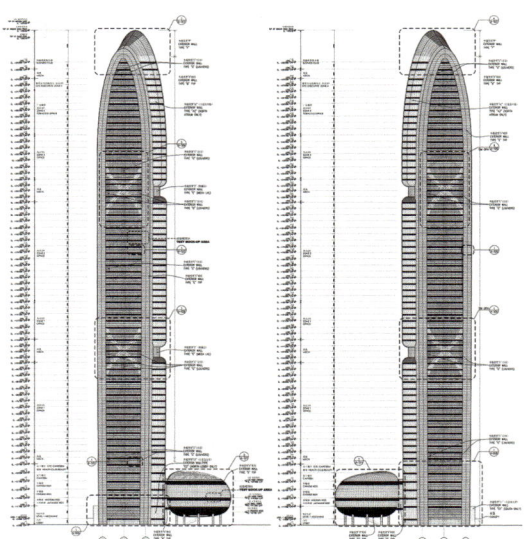

Ost- und Westansicht
Elevation east and west

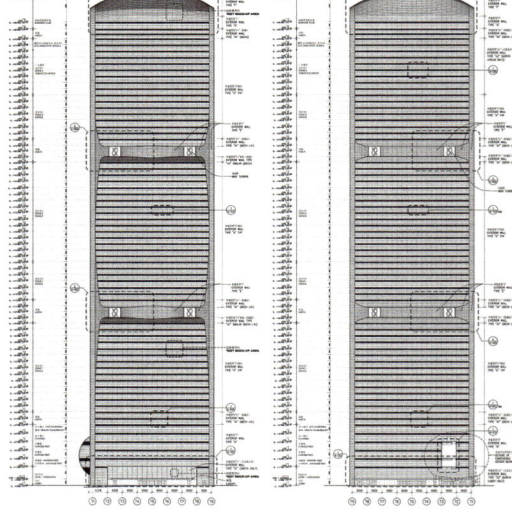

Süd- und Nordansicht
Elevation south and north

Das Verwaltungsgebäude in Pearl River New Town,
einem neuen Geschäftsviertel von Guangzhou, versteht
sich als „Hochhaus des 21. Jahrhunderts". Es ist nicht
nur energieeffizient angelegt, es produziert auch selbst
Strom aus Windkraft. In den Technikgeschossen
befinden sich an der konkav geformten Südseite vier
Öffnungen mit Turbinen, die durch die an Hochhäusern
üblichen Wind-lasten betrieben werden und Energie
erzeugen.

The office building in Pearl River New Town, a new
business district in Guangzhou, sees itself as a
'twenty-first-century highrise'. It is not just energy
efficient in its conception, it also produces its own
electricity through the use of wind power. There are
four openings with turbines on the concave southern
elevation of the service floors, which are driven by the
typical wind forces experienced by highrises, and
which generate energy.

Somdoon Architects
IDEO MORPH 38
Bangkok, Thailand

Architekten **Architects** Somdoon Architects, Bangkok
Bauherr **Client** Anada Development PCL

Höhe **Height**
Ashton Tower 134 m, Skyle Tower 65 m
Geschosse **Floors**
Ashton Tower 32, Skyle Tower 10
Grundstücksfläche **Site area** 5320 m²
Bebaute Fläche **Footprint** Ashton Tower 936 m², Skyle
Tower 757 m²
Nettogeschossfläche **Net floor area** Ashton Tower
26158 m², Skyle Tower 10 885 m²

Konstruktion **Structure** Spannbetonplatten,
vorgefertigte Betonelemente **Post-tensioned slab,
precast concrete elements**
Fertigstellung **Completion** Januar **January** 2013
Nutzung **Use** Wohnen und Restaurant **Residential and
restaurant**
Ökologische Aspekte / Nachhaltigkeit **Ecological
criteria / sustainability** Begrünte Flächen an den
Fassaden dienen als Sonnenschutz; durchgehende
Begrünung der Parkhausfassaden; natürliche
Durchlüftung auf den Verteilerebenen.
**Green façades to provide protection from the sun;
all-over green façades for the multi-storey car park;
natural ventilation on the concourse levels.**

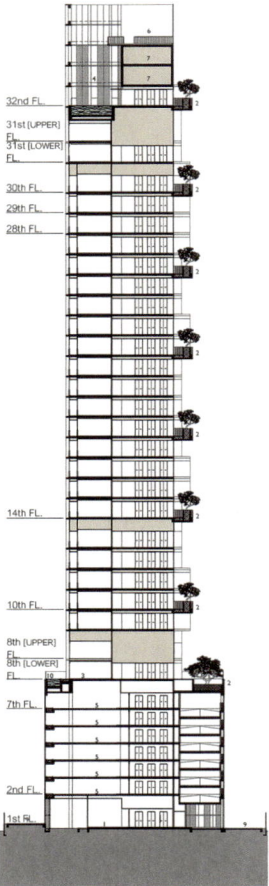

Schnitt **Section** Ashton Tower

Grundriss 8. Obergeschoss Ashton Tower
Floor plan of 8th storey: Ashton Tower

Ideo Morph 38 ist ein Komplex aus einem 32-
geschossigen und einem 10-geschossigen Wohnhochhaus. Für den Standort in einem durchgrünten
Villenviertel bedurfte das Projekt der Zustimmung der
Bewohner des umliegenden Viertels. Es kommt ihnen
mit viel Grün entgegen. Die Fassaden bestehen aus
einem unregelmäßigen Stahlgitterwerk, das mit vertikal
bepflanzten Wänden kombiniert ist. Auf den Verteiler-
etagen sind „Himmelsgärten" angelegt und auch das
Dachgeschoss ist begrünt und dient sportlichen
Aktivitäten.

Ideo Morph 38 is a complex consisting of one 32-
storey and one 10-storey residential building. Because
of its location in a district of detached houses with a
lot of green, the project required the acquiescence
of the residents of the surrounding neighbourhood. The
large quantity of plants used in this projects is a
concession to them. The façades consist of an
irregular steel grid combined with living walls. The
concourse levels have 'sky gardens' and the roof
terrace is also covered in plants and is to be used for
sporting activities.

Nominiertes Projekt 2014
Nominated Project 2014

Tago Architects
DUMANKAYA IKON
Istanbul, Türkei **Turkey**

Architekten **Architects** Tago Architects, Istanbul
Bauherr **Client** Dumankaya Construction Inc.

Höhe **Height** 149 m
Geschosse **Floors** 21
Grundstücksfläche **Site area** 16 800 m²
Bebaute Fläche **Footprint** 4000 m²
Nettogeschossfläche **Net floor area** 151 000 m²

Konstruktion **Structure** Stahlbeton **Reinforced concrete**
Fertigstellung **Completion** 2012
Nutzung **Use** Wohnen **Residential**
Ökologische Aspekte / Nachhaltigkeit **Ecological
criteria / sustainability** Erdbebensichere
Stahlbetonkonstruktion; verbesserte Durchlüftung
aufgrund der Aufteilung in drei Türme; Begrünung der
Verbindungsbügel und Terrassen.
Earthquake-proof reinforced concrete structure;
improved ventilation thanks to the division into three
towers; the connecting arms and terraces are covered
in plants.

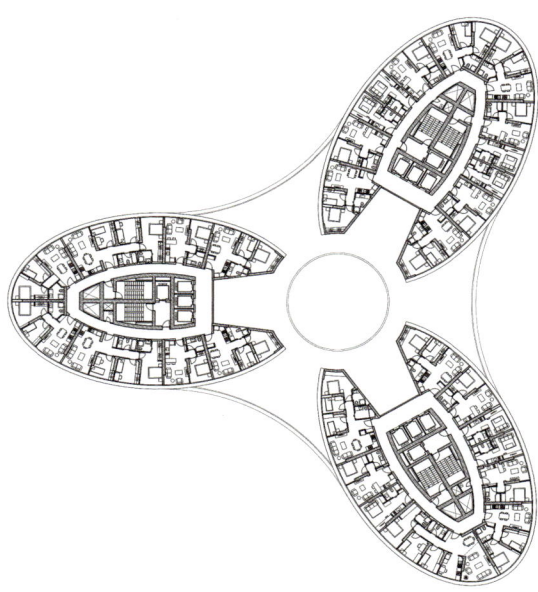

Grundriss Regelgeschoss
Typical floor plan

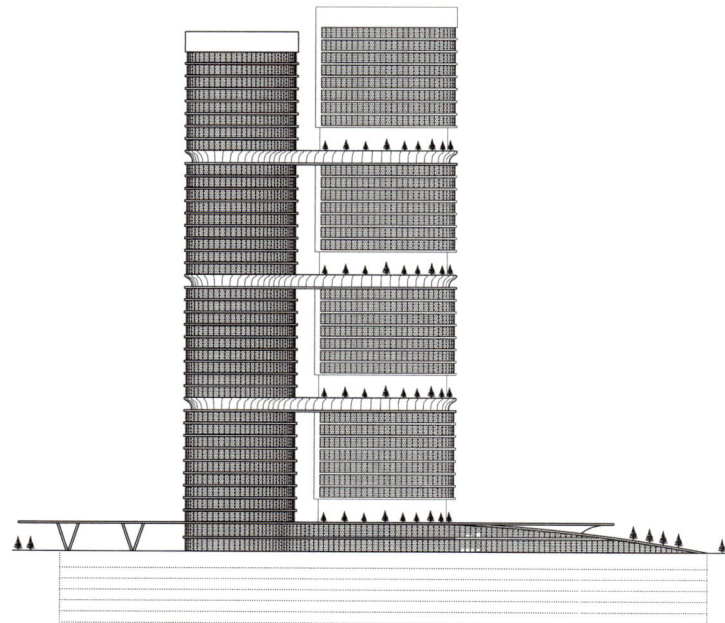

Ansicht
Elevation

Das im Istanbuler Stadtteil Göztepe gelegene
Wohnhochhaus besteht aus drei separaten Türmen,
die durch drei horizontale Verbindungsbügel
zusammengehalten werden. Diese verklammern die
Türme statisch und dienen der Erdbebensicherheit. Sie
sind begrünt, bilden zum Teil hängende Gärten aus
und können von den Bewohnern als offene Brücken
genutzt werden.

The residential highrise in the Göztepe district of
Istanbul consists of three separate towers held
together by three horizontal connecting arms. They
brace the towers from a structural perspective and
make them earthquake proof. They are covered in
plants and have given rise to some hanging gardens.
They can be used by the residents as open walkways.

Nominiertes Projekt 2014
Nominated Project 2014

TEN Arquitectos
MERCEDES HOUSE
New York City, USA

Architekten **Architects** TEN Arquitectos, New York
Bauherr **Client** Two Trees Management

Höhe **Height** 106 m
Geschosse **Floors** 31
Grundstücksfläche **Site area** 8776 m²
Bebaute Fläche **Footprint** 8776 m²
Nettogeschossfläche **Net floor area** 114 323 m²

Konstruktion **Structure** Stahlbeton **Reinforced concrete**
Fertigstellung **Completion** November 2012
Nutzung **Use** Wohnen, Einzelhandel **Residential, retail**
Ökologische Aspekte / Nachhaltigkeit **Ecological
criteria / sustainability** Intensive Dachbegrünung auf
den Terrassen; geringere Verschattung der
Nachbarbebauung durch Reduzierung der Baumassen.
**Roof space and terraces covered in plants; reduced
cubic capacity to reduce the amount of shade cast on
neigh-bouring buildings.**

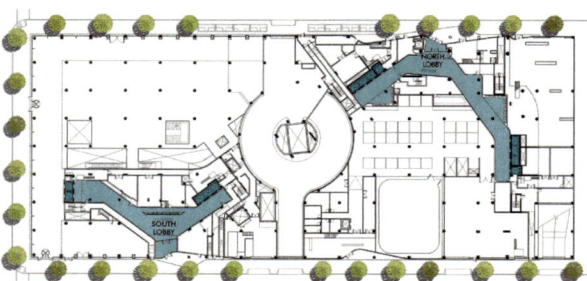

Grundriss Erdgeschoss
Ground floor plan

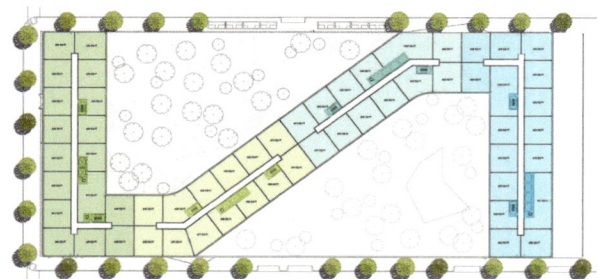

Grundriss Regelgeschosse
Typical floor plan

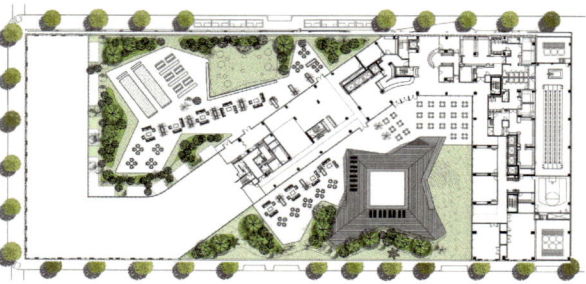

Grundriss Terrassengeschoss
Ground plan for terrace level

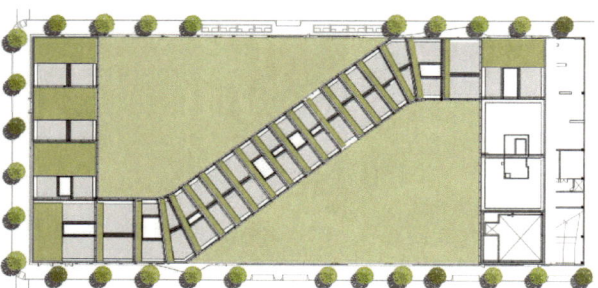

Grundriss Dachterrassen
Ground plan for roof terraces

Der Hochhauskomplex in Midtown Manhattan orientiert
sich in seinen unteren vier Etagen an der Blockrandbebauung. In den darüber liegenden 27 Etagen staffeln
sich die Wohnungen diagonal über das Grundstück
hinweg bis auf eine Höhe von 106 Metern. Durch die
Staffelung erhalten die Wohnungen begrünte
Terrassen. Es entstehen zwei Innenhöfe, die wie die
Wohnungen mehr Tageslicht erhalten, als dies bei einer
geschlossenen Hofbebauung der Fall wäre.

The highrise complex in Midtown Manhattan is geared
on the bottom four floors to the block perimeter. The
27 resi-dential floors above form a diagonal line across
the plot, up to a height of 106 metres. The stepped
design gives the flats their green terraces. The layout
also produces two atria, which, like the flats, receive
more daylight than they would have done in the case
of uniform building on a courtyard.

Nominiertes Projekt 2014
Nominated Project 2014

UN Studio
ARDMORE RESIDENCE
Singapur **Singapore**

Architekten **Architects** UN Studio, Amsterdam
Lokale Architekten **Architects of record** Architects A61,
Singapur **Singapore**
Bauherr **Client** Pontiac Land Group

Höhe **Height** 136 m
Geschosse **Floors** 36
Grundstücksfläche **Site area** 5595 m²
Nettogrundfläche **Net floor area** 15 666m²

Konstruktion **Structure** Beton **Concrete**
Fertigstellung **Completion** September 2013
Nutzung **Use** Wohnen **Residential**
Ökologische Aspekte / Nachhaltigkeit **Ecological
criteria / sustainability** Die Form der Fassaden bietet
Sonnenschutz an den Fensteröffnungen und Balkonen;
Dachbegrünung; Regulierung des Wasserverbrauchs;
natürliche Durchlüftung der Durchgangsbereiche;
energieeffiziente Klimatisierung (VRV).
The shape of the façade provides sun protection at
the window openings and on the balconies; green roofs;
regulated water use; natural ventilation of the corridors
and concourses; energy-efficient air-conditioning
(VRV).

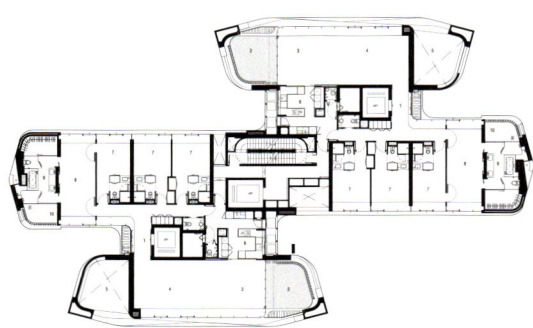

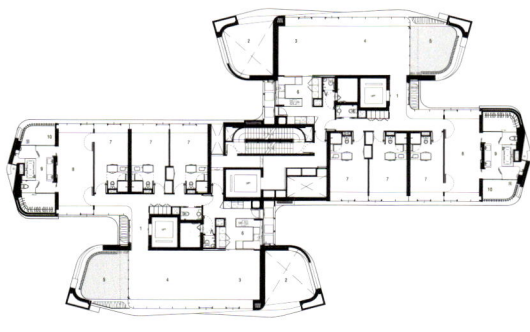

Grundriss 8. und 9. Obergeschoss
Floor plans level 8 and 9

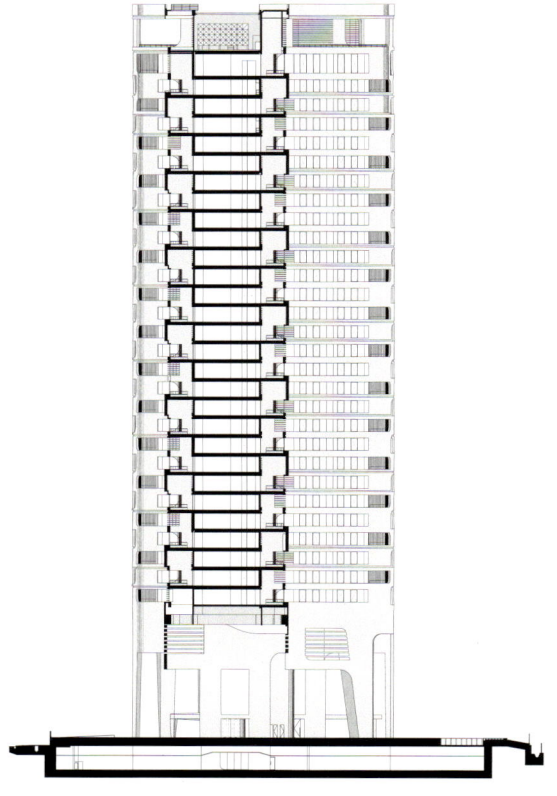

Schnitt
Section

Das in der luxuriösen Umgebung der Orchard Road in
Singapur gelegene Hochhaus spielt nicht nur die
plastischen Möglichkeiten des Betons mit organisch
gerundeten, weiß gefassten Fassaden und Fensteröffnungen aus. Sie entwickeln sich erkerartig aus den
Fassaden heraus und schaffen harmonische Über-
gänge zwischen Innen- und Außenbereichen. Das
Gebäude orientiert sich an der Moderne auch mit
seiner Aufständerung und den fließenden Übergängen
im begrünten Erdgeschossbereich, wo sich elegante
Aufenthaltsqualitäten bieten.

This highrise built in the luxurious surroundings of
Orchard Road in Singapore does more than just take
maximum advantage of the sculptural possibilities of
concrete with its organically shaped, rounded white
façades and window openings. They emerge from the
façades like oriel windows, creating harmonious
transitions between the interior and exterior spaces.
The building echoes Modernism not least thanks to its
being built on stilts and to the flowing transitions in the
green groundfloor area, an elegant place to see and
be seen.

Preisträger Internationaler Hochhaus Preis
Winners of the International Highrise Award
2004 – 2012

Preisträger **Award Winner** 2012
1 Bligh Street
Sydney, Australien **Australia**
Architekten **Architects** ingenhoven architects,
Düsseldorf + Architectus, Sydney
Leitende Architekten **Principal architects** Christoph
Ingenhoven, Ray Brown (Architectus)
Projektarchitekten **Project architects** Martin Reuter
(ingenhoven architects), Mark Curzon (Architectus)
Bauherr **Client** DEXUS Property Group, DEXUS
Wholesale Property Fund, Cbus Property, Sydney

Preisträger **Award Winner** 2010
The Met Bangkok, Thailand
Architekten **Architects** WOHA, Singapur **Singapore**
Assoziierte Architekten **Associated architects** Tandem
Architects 2001 Co. Ltd., Bangkok
Bauherr **Client** Pebble Bay Thailand Co. Ltd., Singapur
Singapore

Preisträger **Award Winner** 2008
Hearst Headquarters New York City, USA
Architekten **Architects** Foster + Partners, London
(Entwurfsplanung **Project designer**); Adamson
Associates, Toronto (Lokale Architekten / Rohbau;
Architects of record / shell and core)
Bauherr **Client** Hearst Corporation, New York City

Preisträger **Award Winner** 2006
Torre Agbar Barcelona, Spanien **Spain**
Architekten **Architects** Ateliers Jean Nouvel, Paris
Bauherr **Client** Layetana Developments, Barcelona

Preisträger **Award Winner** 2004
De Hoftoren Den Haag **The Hague**, Niederlande
Netherlands
Architekten **Architects** Kohn Pedersen Fox Associates
International PA, London
Bauherr **Client** ING Vastgoed, Den Haag **The Hague**

1 Bligh Street Sydney, Australien **Australia**

The Met Bangkok, Thailand

Hearst Headquarters New York City, USA

De Hoftoren Den Haag **The Hague**, Niederlande Netherlands

Torre Agbar Barcelona, Spanien **Spain**

3D/International, Houston TX, USA
Carl B. Stokes Federal Courthouse, Cleveland OH, USA
Einreichung Contribution 2004

ABB Architekten, Frankfurt, Germany
Bocom Financial Towers, Shanghai, China
Einreichung Contribution 2004

Aedas, London, UK
Al Bahr Towers, Abu Dhabi, United Arab Emirates
Nominierung Nomination 2014

Aflalo & Gasperini Arquitectos, São Paulo, Brasil
Ventura Corporate Tower, Rio de Janeiro, Brasil
Nominierung Nomination 2012

Amateur Architecture Studio, Hangzhou, China
Vertical Courtyard, Hangzhou, China
Nominierung Nomination 2008

Dina Ammar – Avraham Curiel Architects, Haifa, Israel
The Sail Tower, Haifa, Israel
Einreichung Contribution 2004

Arc Studio Architecture + Urbanism, Singapore
Pinnacle@Duxton, Singapore
Finalist 2012

Architectus, Sydney, Australia
1 Bligh Street, Sydney, Australia
Preisträger Prize Winner 2012

Arquitectonica International Corporation, Hong Kong
Landmark East, Hong Kong
Nominierung Nomination 2010

Audrius Ambrasas Architects, Vilnius, Lithuania
Europa Tower, Vilnius, Lithuania
Einreichung Contribution 2004

Atkins, Dubai, United Arab Emirates
Bahrain World Trade Center, Manama, Bahrain
Nominierung Nomination 2008

Baumschlager-Eberle, Lustenau, Austria
PopMoma, Beijing, China
Nominierung Nomination 2008

Mario Bellini Architects, Milan, Italia
Neue Deutsche Bank Towers (Revitalization), Frankfurt, Germany
Bes. Anerkennung Special Rec. 2012

Boeri Studio, Milan, Italia
Bosco Verticale, Milan, Italia
Preisträger Prize Winner 2014

Mario Botta Architetto, Mendrisio, Switzerland
Kyobo Gangnam Tower, Seoul, South Korea
Finalist 2004

Building Design (Pvt) Ltd., Colombo, Sri Lanka
HNB Towers, Colombo, Sri Lanka
Einreichung Contribution 2004

Santiago Calatrava LLC, Zurich, Switzerland
HSB Turning Torso, Malmö, Sweden
Finalist 2006

CetraRuddy Architecture, New York, USA
One Madison Park, New York, USA
Nominierung Nomination 2012

Cook + Fox Architects LLP, New York, USA
The Bank of America Tower, New York, USA
Nominierung Nomination 2010

Dam & Partners Architecten, Amsterdam, Netherlands
Maastoren, Rotterdam, Netherlands
Nominierung Nomination 2010

Paul Davis & Partners, London, UK
Grosvenor Place, Hong Kong
Einreichung Contribution 2004

Delugan Meissl Associated Architects, Vienna, Austria
Delugan Meissl Tower, Vienna, Austria
Finalist 2006

Donovan Hill, Brisbane, Australia
Santos Place, Brisbane, Australia
Nominierung Nomination 2010

(desinged by) Erick van Egeraat, Rotterdam, Netherlands
Mercury City Tower, Moscow, Russia
Nominierung Nomination 2014

Ellerbe Becket, Minneapolis MN, USA
Kingdom Centre, Riyadh, Saudi Arabia
Einreichung Contribution 2004

EMBA Estudi Massip-Bosch Architects, Barcelona, Spain
Torre Telefónica Tower, Barcelona, Spain
Nominierung Nomination 2012

Fender Katsalidis Architects, Melbourne, Australia
Eureka Tower, Melbourne, Australia
Nominierung Nomination 2008

Foster + Partners, London, UK
30 St Mary Axe, London, UK
Finalist 2004
Deutsche Bank Place, Sydney, Australia
Nominierung Nomination 2006
Hearst Headquarters, New York, USA
Preisträger Prize Winner 2008
Regent Place, Sydney, Australia
Nominierung Nomination 2008
The Willis Building, London, UK
Nominierung Nomination 2008
Jameson House, Vancouver, Canada
Nominierung Nomination 2012
The Index, Dubai, United Arab Emirates
Nominierung Nomination 2012
The Troika, Kuala Lumpur, Malaysia
Finalist 2012
The Bow, Calgary, Canada
Nominierung Nomination 2014

Studio Gang Architects Ltd., Chicago IL, USA
Aqua Tower, Chicago IL, USA
Finalist 2010

Gatermann + Schossig, Cologne, Germany
KölnTriangle, Cologne, Germany
Nominierung Nomination 2006

Gehry Partners LLP, Los Angeles CA, USA
Eight Spruce Street, New York, USA
Finalist 2012

Gerber Architekten, Dortmund, Germany
RWE Tower, Dortmund, Germany
Nominierung Nomination 2006

Gigon/Guyer Architekten, Zurich, Switzerland
Prime Tower, Zurich, Switzerland
Nominierung Nomination 2012

GKK+Architekten, Berlin, Germany
Hauptverwaltung Süddeutscher Verlag, Munich,
Germany
Nominierung Nomination 2010

gmp Architekten von Gerkan, Maag und Partner,
Hamburg, Germany
Guangzhou Development Central Building, Guangzhou,
China
Nominierung Nomination 2006
Wanda Plaza, Beijing, China
Nominierung Nomination 2008
Neue Deutsche Bank Towers (Revitalization), Frankfurt,
Germany
Bes. Anerkennung Special Rec. 2012

Gruber + Kleine-Kraneburg Architekten, Frankfurt,
Germany
TaunusTurm, Frankfurt, Germany
Nominierung Nomination 2014

Zaha Hadid Architects, London, UK
CMA CGM Head Office Tower, Marseille, France
Nominierung Nomination 2012

T.R.Hamzah & Yeang Sdn.Bhd., Ampang Selanger,
Malaysia
Singapore National Library, Singapore
Nominierung Nomination 2006

Steven Holl Architects, New York, USA
Sliced Porosity Block – Raffles City Chengdu,
Chengdu, China
Finalist 2014

Rafael de La-Hoz Arquitectos, Madrid, Spain
Las Torres de Hércules, Los Barrios, Spain
Nominierung Nomination 2010

ingenhoven architects, Düsseldorf, Germany
Uptown München, Munich, Germany
Nominierung Nomination 2006
Breezé Tower, Osaka, Japan
Nominierung Nomination 2010
1 Bligh Street, Sydney, Australia
Preisträger Prize Winner 2012

Johnson Fain, Los Angeles CA, USA
Constellation Palace, Los Angeles CA, USA
Einreichung Contribution 2004

J.S.K. Internationa Architekten und Ingenieure
GmbH, Frankfurt, Germany
Tornado Tower, Doha, Qatar
Nominierung Nomination 2010

Kallmann Mckinnell & Wood Architects, Boston MA,
USA
Carl B. Stokes Federal Courthouse, Cleveland OH,
USA
Einreichung Contribution 2004

Louis Karlsberger & Associates, Columbus OH, USA
Carl B. Stokes Federal Courthouse, Cleveland OH,
USA
Einreichung Contribution 2004

KCAP Architects & Planners, Rotterdam, Netherlands
The Red Apple, Rotterdam, Netherlands
Nominierung Nomination 2010

Kohn Pedersen Fox Associates, New York, USA
De Hoftoren, The Hague, Netherlands
Preisträger Prize Winner 2004
Roppongi Hills Mori Tower, Tokyo, Japan
Einreichung Contribution 2004
Adia Headquarters, Abu Dhabi, United Arab Emirates
Nominierung Nomination 2008
International Commerce Center, Hong Kong
Nominierung Nomination 2008
Shanghai World Financial Center, Shanghai, China
Finalist 2010
Ventura Corporate Tower, Rio de Janeiro, Brasil
Nominierung Nomination 2012

KSP Jürgen Engel Architekten, Frankfurt, Germany
WestendDuo, Frankfurt, Germany
Bes. Anerkennung Special Rec. 2008
Palais Quartier Office Tower, Frankfurt, Germany
Nominierung Nomination 2010

Kuwabara Payne McKenna Blumberg Architects,
Toronto, Canada
Manitoba Hydro Place, Winnipeg, Canada
Nominierung Nomination 2010

C.Y. Lee & Partners, Taipei, Taiwan
Taipei 101, Taipei, Taiwan
Nominierung Nomination 2006

John Lee / Michael Timchula Architects, New York,
USA
Shenzhen World Trade Center, Shenzhen, China
Einreichung Contribution 2004

Studio Daniel Libeskind, New York, USA
Reflections at Keppel Bay, Singapore
Nominierung Nomination 2012

MAD Architects, Beijing, China
Absolute World Towers, Mississauga, Canada
Finalist 2012
Sheraton Huzhou Hot Spring Resort, Huzhou, China
Nominierung Nomination 2014

Prof. Christoph Mäckler Architekten, Frankfurt, Germany
OpernTurm, Frankfurt, Germany
Nominierung Nomination 2010
Zoofenster – Waldorf Astoria Berlin, Berlin, Germany
Nominierung Nomination 2014

Mass Studies, Seoul, South Korea
Missing Matrix Building, Seoul, South Korea
Finalist 2008
S-trenue: Bundle Matrix, Seoul, South Korea
Nominierung Nomination 2010

Mecanoo Architecten, Rotterdam, Netherlands
Montevideo, Rotterdam, Netherlands
Finalist 2006

Mitsubishi Jisho Sekkei Inc., Tokyo, Japan
Breezé Tower, Osaka, Japan
Nominierung Nomination 2010

Ian Moore Architects, Manchester, UK
Air Apartments, Broadbeach/Queensland, Australia
Nominierung Nomination 2008

Morger & Degelo, Marques, Basel, Switzerland
Basler Messeturm/Basel, Switzerland
Einreichung Contribution 2004

Murphy/Jahn Architects, Chicago IL, USA
Post Tower, Bonn, Germany
Einreichung Contribution 2004
Highlight Towers, Munich, Germany
Nominierung Nomination 2006
Veer Towers, Las Vegas, USA
Nominierung Nomination 2012

MVSA – Meyer en Van Schooten Architecten, Amsterdam, Netherlands
New Babylon, The Hague, Netherlands
Nominierung Nomination 2012

Ateliers Jean Nouvel, Paris, France
Torre Agbar, Barcelona, Spain
Preisträger Prize Winner 2006
Doha Tower, Doha, Qatar
Nominierung Nomination 2014
One Central Park, Sydney, Australia
Finalist 2014
Renaissance Barcelona Fira Hotel, Barcelona, Spain
Finalist 2014

Novotny Mähner Assoziierte, Offenbach, Germany
Gallileo, Frankfurt, Germany
Einreichung Contribution 2004

OMA Office for Metropolitan Architecture, Rotterdam/Beijing, Netherlands/China
TVCC – Television Cultural Center, Beijing, China
Finalist 2008
Shenzhen Stock Exchange, Shenzhen, China
Nominierung Nomination 2010
CCTV Headquarters, Beijing, China
Nominierung Nomination 2014
De Rotterdam, Rotterdam, Netherlands
Finalist 2014

Pei Cobb Freed & Partners Architects LLP, New York, USA
Torre Espacio, Madrid, Spain
Nominierung Nomination 2008

Pelli Clarke Pelli Architects, New Haven CT, USA
Two International Finance Center, Hong Kong
Nominierung Nomination 2006
Torre Costanera, Santiago, Chile
Nominierung Nomination 2014

Perkins + Will, Chicago IL, USA
235 West Van Buren, Chicago IL, USA
Nominierung Nomination 2010

Roberto Perez-Guerras Architects, Madrid, Spain
Neguri Gane, Benidorm, Spain
Einreichung Contribution 2004

Dominique Perrault Architecture, Paris, France
ME Barcelona Hotel, Barcelona, Spain
Nominierung Nomination 2010
Fukoku Tower, Osaka, Japan
Nominierung Nomination 2012
DC Tower I, Vienna, Austria
Nominierung Nomination 2014

Renzo Piano Building Workshop, Paris, France
New York Times Building, New York, USA
Finalist 2008
The Shard London Bridge Tower, London, UK
Nominierung Nomination 2014

Atelier Christian Portzamparc, Paris, France
One57, New York, USA
Nominierung Nomination 2014

M. M. Posokhin, Moscow, Russia
Mercury City Tower, Moscow, Russia
Nominierung Nomination 2014

R&AS Rubio & Álvarez-Sala, Madrid, Spain
Torre SyV, Madrid, Spain
Nominierung Nomination 2008

Rapp & Rapp, Amsterdam, Netherlands
De Kroon, The Hague, Netherlands
Nominierung Nomination 2014

Reiser + Umemoto, RUR Architecture PC, New York, USA
O-14, Dubai, United Arab Emirates
Nominierung Nomination 2010

Research Architecture Design Ltd., Hong Kong
SK Telecom Headquarters, Seoul, South Korea
Nominierung Nomination 2006

Rocco Design Architects Ltd., Hong Kong
One Beijing Road, Hong Kong
Einreichung Contribution 2004

Richard Rogers Partnership, London, UK
Hesperia Hotel and Conference Center, L'Hospitalet/Barcelona, Spain
Nominierung Nomination 2008

Rogers Stirk Harbour + Partners, London, UK
8 Chifley Square, Sydney, Australia
Nominierung Nomination 2014
The Leadenhall, London, UK
Nominierung Nomination 2014

Buro Ole Scheeren, Beijing, China
CCTV Headquarters, Beijing, China
Nominierung Nomination 2014

schneider + schumacher, Frankfurt, Germany
Westhafen Tower, Frankfurt, Germany
Einreichung Contribution 2004
Silver Tower (Revitalisation) Frankfurt, Germany
Nominierung Nomination 2010

Harry Seidler and Associates, Sydney, Australia
The Cove, Sydney, Australia
Finalist 2004
Riparian Plaza, Brisbane, Australia
Nominierung Nomination 2006
Meriton Tower, Sydney, Australia
Nominierung Nomination 2008

Ian Simpson Architects, Manchester, UK
Beetham Hilton Tower, Manchester, UK
Nominierung Nomination 2008
Holloway Circus, Birmingham, UK
Nominierung Nomination 2008

Skidmore, Owings & Merrill LLP, Chicago IL, USA
Tower Palace III, Seoul, South Korea
Nominierung Nomination 2006
7 World Trade Center, New York, USA
Nominierung Nomination 2008
Burj Khalifa, Dubai, United Arab Emirates
Bes. Anerkennung Special Rec. 2010
The Broadgate Tower, London, UK
Nominierung Nomination 2010
Trump International Hotel & Tower, Chicago IL, USA
Nominierung Nomination 2010
Tianjin Global Financial Center, Tianjin, China
Nominierung Nomination 2012
Cayan Tower, Dubai, United Arab Emirates
Nominierung Nomination 2014
Pearl River Tower, Guangzhou, China
Nominierung Nomination 2014

Somdoon Architects, Bangkok, Thailand
Ideo Morph 38, Bangkok, Thailand
Nominierung Nomination 2014

Steidle + Partner, Munich, Germany
Chaowei Men, Beijing, China
Nominierung Nomination 2008

Robert A. M. Stern Architects LLP, New York, USA
Comcast Center, Philadelphia PA, USA
Nominierung Nomination 2010

Tabanlioglu Architects, Istanbul, Turkey
Sapphire, Istanbul, Turkey
Nominierung Nomination 2012

Tago Architects, Istanbul, Turkey
Dumankaya Ikon, Istanbul, Turkey
Nominierung Nomination 2014

Tange Associates, Tokyo, Japan
Mode Gakuen Cocoon Tower, Tokyo, Japan
Finalist 2010
One Raffles Place Tower 2, Singapore
Nominierung Nomination 2012

Tectum Architects, Riga, Latvia
Hansabanka Central Office, Riga, Latvia
Nominierung Nomination 2006

TEN Arquitectos, New York, USA
Mercedes House, New York, USA
Nominierung Nomination 2014

TFP Farrells, London, UK
KK 100, Shenzhen, China
Nominierung Nomination 2012

UN Studio, Amsterdam, Netherlands
Ardmore Residence, Singapore
Nominierung Nomination 2014

Valode & Pistre Architects, Paris, France
T1 Tower, Paris, France
Nominierung Nomination 2010

Wilkinson Eyre Architects, London, UK
Guangzhou International Finance Center, Guangzhou, China
Nominierung Nomination 2012

Frank Williams & Associates, New York, USA
Mercury City Tower, Moscow, Russia
Nominierung Nomination 2014

Wingårdh Arkitektenkontor AB, Gothenburg, Sweden
Victoria Tower, Stockholm, Sweden
Nominierung Nomination 2012

WOHA Architects, Singapore
Newton Suites, Singapore
Finalist 2008
The Met, Bangkok, Thailand
Preisträger Prize Winner 2010

Riken Yamamoto & Field Shop, Yokohama, Japan
Jian Wai Soho, Beijing, China
Finalist 2006

Carlos Zapata Studio, New York, USA
Bitexco Financial Tower, Ho Chi Minh City, Vietnam
Nominierung Nomination 2012

Impressum Projektkoordination
Imprint Project Coordination

Stadt Frankfurt am Main
DAM Deutsches Architekturmuseum:
Peter Cachola Schmal, Direktor, **Director**
Peter Körner, Koordination, **Coordination**
Susanne Lehmann, Koordination/Partnerbetreuung und
Öffentlichkeitsarbeit, **Coordination/Partner Support,
Public Relations**
Inka Plechaty, Jacqueline Brauer, Verwaltung,
Administration

Dezernat Kultur und Wissenschaft:
Antje Runge, Referentin für Presse- und
Öffentlichkeitsarbeit, **Head of Press and Public
Relations, Culture and Science Department**

DekaBank:
Silke Schuster-Müller, Leiterin Gesellschaftliches
Engagement, **Head of Social Concerns**
Valery Trosdorf, Gesellschaftliches Engagement, **Social
Concerns**
Björn Korschinowski, Leiter Externe Kommunikation,
Head of External Communication
Marika Beuthan, Miriam Breh, Pressestelle, **Press
Office**

Medienpartner **Media partner**

Impressum Katalog
Imprint Catalogue

Dieser Katalog erscheint anlässlich der Ausstellung
„Best Highrises 2014/15" des Deutschen
Architekturmuseums, Dezernat Kultur und
Wissenschaft, Stadt Frankfurt am Main vom
20. November 2014 bis zum 1. Februar 2015 im
Deutschen Architekturmuseum, Frankfurt am Main.
**This catalogue accompanies the exhibition "Best High-
rises 2014/15", organized by the Deutsches
Architekturmuseum, Department of Culture and
Science, Frankfurt am Main, Germany, taking place
from 20 November 2014 till 1 February 2015 at
Deutsches Architekturmuseum, Frankfurt am Main.**

© Prestel Verlag, Munich · London · New York 2014
www.prestel.de
Das Copyright für die Texte liegt bei den Autoren.
**The copyright on the texts is held by the respective
author.**
Das Copyright für die Abbildungen liegt bei den
Fotografen / Inhabern der Bildrechte.
**The copyright on the pictures is held by the respective
photographer / holder of the picture rights.**
Das Copyright für die Gestaltung liegt beim
Grafikdesigner.
**The copyright on the layout is held by the graphic
designer.**

Prestel Verlag, **Munich**
A member of Verlagsgruppe Random House GmbH

Prestel Verlag
Neumarkter Straße 28
81673 **Munich**
Tel. +49 (0)89 4136-0
Fax +49 (0)89 4136-2335
www.prestel.de

Prestel Publishing Ltd.
14-17 Wells Street
London W1T 3PD
Tel. +44 (0)20 7323-5004
Fax +44 (0)20 7323-0271

Prestel Publishing
900 Broadway, Suite 603
New York, NY 10003
Tel. +1 (212) 995-2720
Fax +1 (212) 995-2733
www.prestel.com

Die Deutsche Nationalbibliothek verzeichnet diese
Publikation in der Deutschen Nationalbibliografie;
detaillierte bibliografische Daten sind im Internet über
http://www.dnb.de abrufbar. / **The Deutsche Bibliothek
holds a record of this publication in the Deutsche
Nationalbibliografie; detailed bibliographical data can
be found under: http://www.dnb.de**

The Library of Congress Cataloguing-in-Publication
data is available
British Library Cataloguing-in-Publication Data: a
catalogue record for this book is available from the
British Library

Herausgeber **Editors**
Peter Körner, Peter Cachola Schmal

Redaktion **Editing**
Peter Körner

Projekttexte **Project texts**
Dr. Corinne Elsesser

Lektorat (deutsch) **Copyediting (German)**
Willfried Baatz

Lektorat (englisch) **Copyediting (english)**
Michael Scuffil

Übersetzungen Deutsch – Englisch
Translations German – English
Josephine Cordero Sapien
Jeremy Gaines, Frankfurt am Main
Mary Dobrian

Übersetzungen Englisch – Deutsch
Translations English – German
Ulrike Bischoff

Endkorrektorat **Proofreading**
Ute Thomsen

Gestaltung **Graphic Design**
Joachim Mildner, Köln / Zürich

Umschlagfoto **Cover**
Kirsten Bucher, Frankfurt am Main

Koordination im Verlag **Coordination publishing house**
Constanze Holler

Herstellung **Production**
Andrea Cobré

Lithografie **Lithography**
farbo prepress, Köln

Druck und Bindung **Printing and binding**
Passavia Druckservice GmbH & Co. KG, Passau

Papier **Paper**
Verlagsgruppe Random House FSC® N001967
The FSC®-certified paper Hello Fat matt
was supplied by Deutsche Papier

ISBN 978-3-7913-5400-2

Impressum Ausstellung
Imprint Exhibition

Direktor **Director** DAM
Peter Cachola Schmal

Kurator **Curator**
Peter Körner

Projekttexte **Project texts**
Dr. Corinne Elsesser

Layout Wettbewerbstafeln **Layout submission panels**
Deserve Gbr Raum und Medien Design, Wiesbaden /
Berlin, Mario Lorenz

Ausstellungsgrafik **Graphic design of the exhibition**
Deserve Gbr Raum und Medien Design, Wiesbaden /
Berlin, Mario Lorenz

Leitung Ausstellungsaufbau **Director exhibit setup**
Christian Walter

Ausstellungsaufbau und Hängung **Exhibit setup**
Enrico Hirsekorn, Paolo Brunino, Achim Müller-Rahn,
Valerian Wolenik, Marina Barry, Angela Tonner, Beate
Voigt, Eike Laeuen, Gerhard Winkler, Herbert Warmuth,
Michael Reiter

Registrar **Registrar**
Wolfgang Welker

Modelle **Models**
Stefano Boeri Architetti, Mailand **Milan**
Office for Metropolitan Architecture, Rotterdam
Ribas Ribas Arquitectos, Barcelona
Steven Holl Architects, New York

Modellrestaurierung **Model restoration**
Christian Walter

Sekretariat und Verwaltung **Administrative staff**
Inka Plechaty, Jacqueline Brauer

Öffentlichkeitsarbeit **Public Relations**
Susanne Lehmann, Brita Köhler

Gestaltung Printmedien **Graphic design printmedia**
Gardeners, Frankfurt am Main

Gestaltung **Graphic design** Internationaler Hochhaus
Preis **The International Highrise Award**
Joachim Mildner, Köln / Zürich **Cologne / Zurich**

Veranstaltungsorganisation **Event organization**
Jazzunique, Frankfurt am Main
Jesper Götsch, Josephine Würl

Danksagung für großzügige finanzielle Unterstützung
Acknowledgements for generous funding
DekaBank, Partner des **of** DAM
Stifter des Internationalen Hochhaus Preises und
Sponsor der Ausstellung **Sponsor of The
International Highrise Award and the exhibition**

Mit besonderem Dank an
With special acknowledgements to
Elizabeth Acas, Michaela Busenkell, Romina
Casagrande, Murat Çavuşoğlu, Fatma Cesur, Elena V.
Davidenko, Jos Dekker, Ellen Denk, Pan Di, Sandrine
Gill, Michelle Gulickx, Anne-Cecile Guthmann, Kathrin
Hasskamp, Yvette Higson, Nicole Hoffmann, Julia van
den Hout, Charlotte Jean, Anisha Jogani, Anne-Marie
Koot, Anastasia Kucherova, Vicki Macgregor, Julie
Maniere, Angeliue Mans, Azzurra Muzzonigro, Arturo
Osorio, Kevin Ou, Tae-Ry Park, Etienne Pierres,
Nicolas Plump, Rachel Prance, Fiona Qi, Birgit Rapp,
Katie Rathbone, Stefan Redfern,Elena Spadavecchia,
Sarah Simpkin, Andrea Steele, Shary Tawil, Tammy
Xie, Elettra Zadra

Abbildungsnachweise **Picture Credits**

Bosco Verticale, Mailand **Milan**
Foto **Photo** Kirsten Bucher, Frankfurt

Gewinner **Prize Winner** 2014
3-7 Kirsten Bucher; 8 Boeri Studio; 9, 11 Kirsten
Bucher

Essay Peter Cachola Schmal
12 Hines Italia, 13 Kirsten Bucher; 15 oben **top** Paolo
Rosselli, unten **bottom** Kirsten Bucher; 17 oben **top**
Kirsten Bucher, unten links **bottom left** Herzog & De
Meuron, unten rechts **bottom right** Peter Körner/DAM;
19 oben **top** Marco Garofalo, unten **bottom** Peter
Körner/DAM

Text Hines Italia
21 Kirsten Bucher; 23 oben **top** Marco Garofalo, unten
bottom Peter Körner/DAM

Essay Laura Gatti
25, 26 Boeri Studio; 28 links **left** Arup, rechts **right**
Peter Cachola Schmal/DAM

Besichtigung **Visiting** Bosco Verticale
29 Kirsten Bucher, mitte rechts **center right** Peter
Cachola Schmal

Vorwort **Preface**
32-34 Olaf Hermann; 35 Peter Körner/DAM

Finalisten **Finalists** 2014
38 Steven Holl Architects; 39 oben **top** Shu He,
bottom unten Hufton & Crow; 40 oben rechts **top
right** Hufton & Crow, oben links **top left** Steven Holl
Architects, unten links **bottom left** Hufton & Crow,
unten rechts **bottom right** Steven Holl Architects;
41 links **left** Steven Holl Architects, rechts **right** Shu He;
42 Iwan Baan; 43 oben **top** Iwan Baan, unten links
bottom left Hufton & Crow, unten rechts **bottom right**
Iwan Baan
45 links oben **top left** John Gollings, unten **links
bottom left** Simon Wood, rechts **right** Simon Wood;
46 oben **top** Ateliers Jean Nouvel, unten links **bottom
left** Ateliers Jean Nouvel, unten rechts **bottom right**
Simon Wood; 47 Simon Wood; 48 Murray Fredericks;
49 oben links **top left** & oben mitte **top center** Simon
Wood, oben rechts **top right** & unten **bottom** Murray
Fredericks; Alle Fotos von **All photos by** John Gollings,
Murray Fredericks, Simon Wood: courtesy of Frasers
Property and Sekisui House
51, 52 Roland Halbe; 53 Ateliers Jean Nouvel;
54,55 Roland Halbe
56, 57 Ossip van Duivenbode; 58 oben **top** Ossip van
Duivenbode, courtesy of OMA, unten **bottom** OMA;
59 links **left** OMA, rechts **right** Dave Pronk; 60 oben
links **top left** Ossp van Duivenbode, oben rechts **top
right** Klaas Vermaas, unten links **bottom left** OMA,
unten rechts **bottom right** Roel Vincken; 61 oben links
top left & Ossip van Duivenbode, courtesy of OMA,
oben rechts **top right** Ossip van Duivenbode, mitte
center Ossip van Duivenbode, unten **bottom** OMA

Nominierte Projekte **Nominated Projects** 2014
62 Aedas; 63 Christian Richters; 64 (designed by)
Erick van Egeraat; 65 Mercury Group; 66 Foster &
Partners; 67 Nigel Young, Foster & Partners; 68 Gruber +
Kleine-Kraneburg Architekten; 69 Klaus Helbig; 70
MAD Architects; 71 Xia Zhi; 72 Prof Christoph Mäckler
Architekten; 73 oben **top** H.G. Esch, unten **bottom**
Christian Richters; 74 Ateliers Jean Nouvel; 75 Chen
Su, CSCEC; 76 OMA; 77 Buro Ole Scheeren; 78 Pelli
Clarke Pelli Architects; 79 oben **top** & unten links
bottom left Pablo Blanco, unten rechts **bottom right**
skyscrapercity.com/Mrzer0; 80 Dominique Perrault
Architecture; 81 oben links **top left** Dominique Perrault
Architecture, oben rechts **top right** & unten **bottom**
Michael Nagl; 82 Renzo Piano Building Workshop;
83 Michel Denancé; 84 Atelier Christian de Portzamparc;
85 oben **top** Atelier Christian de Portzamparc, unten
links **bottom left** Extell, unten rechts **bottom right**
Etienne Pierres; 86 Rapp & Rapp; 87 oben **top** &
unten links **bottom left** Kim Zwarts, unten rechts
bottom right Henk de Jong; 88 Rogers Stirk Harbour
and Partners; 89 oben **top** & unten links **bottom left**
Brett Boardman, unten rechts **bottom right** Rogers Stirk
Harbour and Partners; 90 Rogers Stirk Harbour and
Partners; 91 Paul Raftery; 92 SOM; 93 Tom Griffith;
94 SOM; 95 Tom Griffith; 96 Somdoon Architects;
97 oben links **top left** Chaichoompol Vathakanon,
oben rechts **top right** Spaceshift Studio, unten
bottom W Workspace; 98 Tago Architects;
99 Cemal Emden; 100 TEN Arquitectos; 101 oben **top**
Evan Joseph, unten links **bottom left** TEN Arquitectos,
unten rechts **bottom right** Two Trees; 102 UN Studio;
103 Iwan Baan

Preisträger IHP 2004-2012
Winners of the IHA 2004-2012
104 oben **top** H.G.Esch, unten **bottom** Kirsten Bucher;
105 oben links **top left** Chuck Choi, oben rechts **top
right** H.G. Esch, unten Philippe Ruault